CW00665946

HOW TO RUN A
Part-Time
Business

Also by Barrie Hawkins:

THINK UP A BUSINESS (with Grant Bage)
MAKING CONTRACTS (with Grant Bage)

HOW TO RUN A
Part-Time
Business

TURN YOUR IDEAS
INTO BUSINESS
SUCCESS

BARRIE HAWKINS

PIATKUS

To DMH

© 1993 Barrie Hawkins

First published in 1993 by
Judy Piatkus (Publishers) Ltd of
5 Windmill Street, London W1P 1HF

The moral right of the author has been asserted

A catalogue record for this book is
available from the British Library

ISBN 0-7499-1271-5 (hb)
      0-7499-1236-7 (pb)

Edited by Carol Franklin
Designed by Sue Ryall

Set in Compugraphic Baskerville 11½/13 pt. by
Action Typesetting Limited, Gloucester
Printed and bound in Great Britain by
Biddles Ltd, Guildford & King's Lynn

C O N T E N T S

WHAT SHOULD YOU DO?

CHAPTER ONE

A part-time business is ideal for...

Everyone who wants to have their own part-time business. You can have the security of regular income from the profits your business generates. You can build an asset for yourself and enjoy the satisfaction of putting your spare time – or time you now waste? – to interesting use. However, a part-time business is not ideal for everybody.

> *Mr Automaton's job is tedious and boring. But his attitude is, 'What does it matter what you do so long as you get paid at the end of the month?' He spends his evenings watching television ('A load of rubbish,' he says). He is contented with his lifestyle, although he wouldn't mind being better off ('Who wouldn't?' he says), but he is not prepared to do anything to achieve that.*

An exaggerated portrait, or is it? Cast your mind over your friends and acquaintances, and people you have known in the past... Perhaps, as a customer, you have met such a person? Or was he a bureaucrat you had to deal with?

If you recognise this as a portrait of yourself then there seems little point in reading on.

However, a part-time business is ideal for you if:

- you are looking for a source of extra income; or

- you need some income to finance your studies; or

- you plan to set up a full-time business in the future, but would like to test the water first; or

- you are looking for a new interest/pastime; or

- you are already in business and would like to bolt on another business activity; or

- this idea appeals to you – spending perhaps a couple of days each week in one occupation and a couple of days engaged in some other interest; or

- in these uncertain times, you would like something to fall back on in case you lose your job; or

- you need a source of income but have only limited time due to commitments/other interests; or

- you'd like a new challenge in your life; or

- you're one of the growing band of individuals prepared to opt for a smaller income in return for more time to give to things in life other than working to pay the mortgage; or

- you have retired – perhaps taken early retirement – and have lurched from working for most of the day to doing no work at all. Now you have the time to...

To what? In Chapters 3, 4 and 5 you will find a range of techniques and approaches to generate business ideas suitable for a part-time operation.

But first, in Chapter 2, we scrutinise the obstacles you might face in operating part time and you will learn how these can be overcome.

This book assumes no prior knowledge of launching or running a business. You can start here from scratch, to gain the knowledge and skills possessed by those who run a successful, profitable, small business.

The book is based upon experience. First, there is my experience in setting up and running my own part-time business. Second, there are the experiences of others, who have attended my business start-up courses, from which I have learned.

Many people are uncertain what steps to take first, to achieve 'lift off'. And a surprising number of people have a tendency to delay matters – are *you* inclined to put things off? This book's SIX DAY ACTION PLAN will help get you on to that launch pad.

The benefits of operating part time

- If you have not operated your own business before, this mode of operation provides you with **an opportunity to dip your toe in the water** to see if you like it – and to see if you are any good at it – without running the risk of throwing up your existing income.

- Or perhaps you could operate part time to **test out a particular business idea.** In a flash of inspiration you've come up with this new gizmo or you've suddenly spotted this gap in the market. But, once your pulse has stopped racing, the doubts begin to creep in. Don't fall into the temptation of saying to yourself, 'I'll have a go at that one day' and then putting it aside; instead, work out ways of having a go at it *now* by fitting it around your existing commitments. Perhaps you don't have enough confidence in your idea, or maybe not enough experience of business, to throw up a career, but my experience is that if you freeze your brilliant idea now, almost certainly you'll never defrost it. It will be just another one of those regrets that creeps into your mind from time to time as the birthdays come and go . . .

- If you plan to run your part-time business alongside your full-time job, there is **not at all the same financial risk.** This in turn brings the huge advantage that almost certainly the early days (at least) will be far less stressful.

  This book is not a sales brochure trying to sell you a part-time business opportunity: my wish is for you to weigh up both the pros and the cons, and then decide whether the proposition is for you. So here I must remind you that no business is completely insulated from stress: running a scaled-down operation, you will still have a certain amount of aggravation to deal with – unless you have perfect suppliers and customers! Like anybody else running a business, you are where the buck stops: you can't pass the complaining customer on to another department.

  And if your business idea is one that needs high levels of perseverance and determination to succeed, less pressure can mean you do not boil up enough of that determination. But on the other hand, if you still have income from another source, this may allow you to persevere with the business. Possibly you would be able to subsidise your fledgling enterprise beyond the stage of the individual who, having burned their boats, would have been forced to call a halt. Your list of minus points has, however, to include this piece of reality: if you need to borrow money from the bank to launch your enterprise, the manager may feel that operating part time demonstrates a lack of commitment to the project. If the manager bounces this point across to you at the interview, you can counter it with the perseverance point.

● Your little business may be able to **stay below the VAT threshold**. To those who have not experienced personally the burden placed upon a small business by the accounting complexities and requirements of value added tax, this may appear a minor benefit. But it is even possible for the VAT factor to weigh so heavily that the small business feels it is no longer worth going on. This might not be because of the hours spent in bookkeeping or the dreaded visit from the VAT collector, but due to the implications for profitability. A business is required to register for VAT and charge the tax to customers when its turnover reaches a specified level. Some years ago I knew of a small business operating on profit margins that were very modest, but sufficient to justify the continued existence of the business in the light of the proprietor's financial needs. Experience proved that prices were pegged at the level the market would bear and that an increase in prices would cause sales to drop to an unprofitable level. So when turnover reached the VAT registration level, the tax could not be added on to the price paid by the customer, yet nor could it be absorbed into the existing price, since this would eat damagingly into profits. That particular business registered for VAT and then closed down two months later. If your business does not have the turnover of a full-time enterprise it may well be that you will not reach, or will choose not to reach, the VAT threshold.

- Huge numbers of people who long to set up in business cannot think of a business to set up: they cannot come up with the right business idea. So they never do set up doing their own thing. A pity. Instead of waiting for the Big Idea to flash into their mind – the business opportunity that is so exactly right that it will definitely work and they can throw up their job – this person should consider setting up something that falls short of their ideal but which they **could set up NOW**. Is this person you? Is your ambition eventual full-time self-employment? You could wait and wait and wait for the business scheme that exactly fits your requirements. You may still be waiting when the time comes that you no longer have the energy or capabilities to carry it out. Without doubt, once you are in business, opportunities come to you because you *are* in business that you would not otherwise have come across. You will be talking to suppliers, meeting other people in the same trade, dealing with professional advisers such as your accountant, who happens to have a client who is looking for a partner for his expanding small business...

It is very feasible

I have met a great number of people who want their own business. I discovered that a surprisingly high number of these potential entrepreneurs equated owning a business with full-time commitment. Some who had considered a part-time business felt that a scaled-down operation would be amateurish, that somehow it was 'playing at business'. Why should this be so? If small is beautiful, then very small can be very beautiful. A miniature can be as great a work of art as any life-size portrait. Provided you do not over-stretch your resources, a less than full-time commitment does not equate with an inferior product. Plenty of full-time businesses are run in an amateurish fashion, falling well short of what they should be providing to customers: what counts is motivation, and the quality of effort and skills that you put into your business. Your fewer number of hours may be more productive and of more worth than the full-time efforts of the incompetent manager.

Are you in doubt as to whether you have enough time for this project? Keep a log of how you spend each fifteen minutes over the next seven days. It may be an unpleasant surprise to discover how much time you have spent which, on reflection, could have been better spent in other ways. How much time have you spent watching television programmes which afterwards you feel weren't worth watching? And how much time is frittered away, almost without knowing it, in doing very little? Are your energies and abilities wasted? Sitting in the train on the way home from work, do you waste your energies churning over some matter of office politics or personalities?

If you feel a demanding job, or other responsibilities such as children, drain your resources, you will make the pleasant discovery that your new interest energises you. If your evenings find you slumped in the armchair lethargically reading newspapers full of crime, it may be healthier for you to expend some of that time constructively on a little business you are building. The knowledge that you must find the energy to make up the order that has just come in may encourage you first to take a break for some *proper* relaxation.

The benefits of running a part-time business are on top of the usual benefits that come with small business ownership.

Talk to someone who runs their own successful small business and they may tell you of the pleasure in having built up something from scratch. Another person may tell you how they like the freedom to make their own decisions instead of always being 'bossed about'. Still others will tell you how they've enjoyed the challenge or found it has given them something creative to do that they've enjoyed. They will want to tell you also about the obstacles they have experienced running a small business, and how they overcame them, whereupon you will pay even greater attention.

> The book includes accounts of how six people fared when they set up and ran their own part-time business. Each was new to business and you will profit from their experiences, and their tips.

So what type of business are you going to start?

> Throughout this book you will find a range of relevant, practical tasks to undertake. Here is the first: your Personal Profile.
> Completing this will bring into focus what benefits you wish to derive from your mini-business and help you come up with a suitable business idea.
> Enlist the aid of your family and friends: to find out how others see you and to jog your memory.

PERSONAL PROFILE

1. Why do you want to start your own part-time business?

2. What personal qualities do you have that might help you succeed in your own business?

3. Do you have any weaknesses that could be a disadvantage in running your own business?

4. What skills do you possess?

5. What are your natural abilities?

6. What trades/occupations do you have experience of?

7. What are your hobbies/pastimes?

8. In an average month, how much time do you have to devote to your part-time business?

9. When would you like to be in business?

10. What net monthly income would you like to derive from your part-time business?

CHAPTER TWO

Choosing your business

Let us be realistic: you are not going to be running IBM or ICI.

But what is to be the scale of your planned enterprise?

You have some hours in the course of a week that you can devote to a part-time business. Maybe these are hours which are already going spare; you have time on your hands that you wish to fill productively. How much time you – and others you ask to join with you – can devote to your project is an obvious factor in shaping the type and scale of your business.

If your plans do not match up to the time you have available, perhaps you should consider taking a business partner.

It is often said by professionals who advise on business start-ups, that being in a partnership is not unlike being married. In a full-time business, especially in the early years, the partners may even see more of each other than they do of their spouses. Hopefully this will not happen in a business to which you are giving less than your full-time commitment, but you can still suffer the stresses and strains of a business partnership. As in a marriage, the pervasive pulling power of money can distance the partners, but, unlike a marriage, you will not have pulling in your favour that you are in love with your partner!

Why are you setting up in business?

Your business is to be operated on a part-time basis and that consideration weighs heavily in choosing your field of business activity, but you must also weigh in what is to be the return you are seeking from your business. What you get out of your business will be much more than a financial return. Pause to consider here what you hope your business, no matter how small, will give you in return for the time and abilities you bring to it.

If you were to ask a dozen individual entrepreneurs running their own small business what it is they derive from their activity, you could find a dozen different responses, each person motivated by something different they see and feel in what they are doing.

'I needed an outlet for my creativity.'
'I wanted to build something.'
'I wanted to show my children that I was capable of doing something more than the ironing.'
'I think women are better at business than men and I wanted to help prove it.'
'I don't like the way they do things at work, the way they treat their customers and I feel there must be a better way of doing it.'
'I was fed up with that idiot boss telling me what to do all the time. I wanted to make some decisions of my own.'
'I didn't know if I'd be any good at it but I thought if I didn't try I'd never find out.'
'I wanted to do something!'
'I enjoy it.'

13

'I thought to myself one day, there must be more to life than this, and I ended up setting up my own business.'
'When my husband and I parted I needed to show the world I could do things for myself.'

The ambition of individuals will colour their business plans: you may choose not to set up an ironing service, profitable and in demand though it will be, because it may not greatly change how you are seen by your teenage son.

These are matters of emotion and dreams. Keeping our feet firmly on the ground . . .

Pause for thought

Have you considered whether you have the legal *right* to set up a business?

If you are in employment, it is possible that a clause in your contract of employment prohibits you from carrying on business activities. The prohibition may be absolute or it may be that the clause requires you to obtain the consent of your employer before setting up your business.

A common reaction to this is, 'But I don't have a contract of employment.' If you are an employee, you *do* have a contract, since the relationship of employer and employee is a contractual one: you work under a contract of employment. Perhaps the correct response should have been, 'I do not have a *written* employment contract.' This could well be the case, although the employment protection laws require an employer, if the employee works for more than sixteen hours each week, to set out in writing at least the main terms of the employment.

Even if there is no express provision in your contract preventing you as an employee carrying on a business, the law restricts an employee's *choice* of business activity. The basic principle is that employees should not compete with their employer. In practice, very often the field of business in which the employee wishes to set up is that in which their employer operates, because that is the very field in which the employee has experience.

Perhaps your reaction to this is, 'That's not a problem for me – the reason I want to set up my own business is that I have given up my job.' Or perhaps your desire to have your own part-time business is such that you would consider changing your employment if your present employer were to thwart your ambitions.

It comes as a surprise to many employees to discover that they may not have cut themselves entirely free of their employer's bonds when they wave goodbye for the last time: it is increasingly the practice for a contract of employment, particularly in high-tech industries, and in managerial, supervisory or senior posts, to include a clause prohibiting the employee from setting up in business in competition with their employer after the employee has left their employment. The object of such a clause is to empower the former employer to protect their legitimate interests: the law considers it would be unfair, for example, for the former employee to make use of their knowledge of the employer's research and development. Does your present or a previous contract of employment contain such a clause?

If you are aware of, or uncover, such a clause in your contract, do not take it at face value. All is not lost. Such a clause is only valid and enforceable by the employer to the extent that the court considers it reasonable. If you are in any doubt as to whether a clause resembling those described is a term of your contract or as to the meaning or validity of such a clause, then you must of course take legal advice. You must clarify your position before setting up in business: an employee who breaches such a term can finish up on the receiving end of a court injunction, restraining the employee from continuing their business activities, usually accompanied by a writ claiming compensation and costs.

What suits a part-time operation?

In terms of logistics, realistically what sort of business can you run?

In your choice of activity you must bear in mind some potential constraints. Do not be discouraged by these considerations: depending on your particular circumstances you may be able to manoeuvre round some of them. Bear this in mind also: a part-time business, as we shall see, can have a head-start over its full-time rivals.

1. Would the customers of your prospective business expect round-the-clock service? Or might they require your attention at very short notice? If your business was the maintenance of heating systems, what happens if your customer rings on a freezing winter's morning to say the system has broken down, just after you have left home for your full-time job?

   In fact you may find a solution to this problem in Chapter 10.

2. Is the business one which particularly needs to emphasise a professional image? This could arise where clients are placing heavy reliance on your expertise; it is possible that some of your potential clients may feel that a part-time operation sounds less professional. But do you have to tell them? Of course, if the question

arises you must not directly or indirectly mislead the clients into believing your business is a full-time operation, any more than a new business should misrepresent that it is a long-established one, or a small business mislead as to the scale of its operations, all matters which could give rise to a claim for misrepresentation by a customer. You will observe that we are not far into a book on setting up and running a business before the law has raised its head: two later chapters (Chapters 11 and 13) are devoted to more legal considerations.

On the other hand, that it operates part time may fit in very well with the image you wish to create for your business or with its marketing strategy. Let us suppose that you have decided to place emphasis on value for money or upon a bargain price. A percentage of potential customers will be wary and ask themselves why it is that your prices are below those of the competition. They will wonder if it is because your product is inferior. But quite possibly you are more competitive in the market place due to lower operating overheads, thanks to your part-time operations. Thus, your business being operated part time and not having to carry the overheads of a full-time organisation is of positive benefit to your customers. Letting customers know your business operates part time will, in these circumstances, justify your competitive prices.

3. But your business deals not only with customers: what of your suppliers? It is conceivable that you could receive an adverse reaction when sounding out possible sources of supply: they may, for example, feel that your orders will be too small to justify dealing with your business. If you are operating from home and the supplier's representative is visiting you in your sitting room he might perhaps wonder whether you are in

business full time. But with other suppliers you may be visiting their premises or dealing with them through the post or over the phone and the question of your scale of operations never comes up. In any case, the problem is only likely to arise if you are dealing with Giant Multinational PLC: the overwhelming majority of small and medium-sized businesses will be quite happy to deal with you, providing you are a bona fide trader – which you will be – and not a member of the public trying to get something for his personal use at trade price.

4. Is your business idea one that is going to need commercial premises? The question of accommodation for your business is one we look at in some detail later, in Chapter 8, where we consider how to meet the accommodation requirements of the particular business you have decided to launch. But the question of premises should be taken into account also at this earlier stage, when considering what sort of business to set up. With a part-time business, if your idea is one which will involve you in operations which you cannot manage from home, bear in mind that commercial premises may then be left unattended for a lot of the time, more so than those of other businesses. This could pose security problems.

5. Who will answer the phone? The need to man the office is an issue which all small businesses have to face. Would your business be one in which customers and possibly suppliers make heavy demands of the telephone? For example, would the business be one in which potential customers make their initial contact by phone? By contrast, a mail-order operation may find the number of incoming calls from customers is limited to those raising queries on orders.

The use of telephone answering machines has become much more widespread since the restrictions on their availability were removed in the 1980s, but they are not in all circumstances a complete answer. Business people, such as your suppliers, will be more accustomed to dealing with a telephone answerer than will some members of the public. Some people are reluctant to 'talk to a machine', and a proportion of your customers may become tongue-tied and hesitant if they have to make a 'speech' into the telephone.

If your field of operations is one in which a potential client's perception of the scale of your enterprise is relevant – for example he does not think a 'little person' would have the resources to do the job properly – such a customer may wonder why the telephone is not answered by a member of staff. Possible solution: consider employing, on a part-time basis, someone who is at home all day to answer the telephone; this could give useful employment to a person who is not able to work away from home. Alternatively, it may be that a mother or father who is at home with young children for most of the day would provide sufficient coverage. There are possible complications with this solution: will your telephone minder need detailed product knowledge? Will they need sales expertise? You can probably easily supply the former; are you able to supply the latter? If selling ability is a requirement, advertise for a telephone minder with a sales background.

Dealing with the telephone is a major aspect of the important problem of your general availability to deal with matters. Is your business going to be taking regular deliveries of stock? A small catering service may take daily deliveries of fresh produce: who will receive the goods? It is common for carriers to require a signature before releasing their consignment: whose signature will it be? The obvious solution is that your delivery address does not have to be the same as your office address, so you can arrange for a nearby relative or a neighbour to take delivery of your goods, in return for a small remuneration or some free samples.

6. Consider the aggravation factor. You have already been reminded that running any business involves a willingness to undertake a measure of responsibility and no business will enjoy stress-free operation. Most people are honest and reasonable in their business dealings or nobody could do business, but a small percentage of people are unreasonable, and the occasional customer may be very trying. Some trades, by their nature, involve a greater degree of personal responsibility or pressure than others. If you are already subjected to high levels of these elsewhere, in your regular job for example, too great an additional helping from your spare-time business may prove such a burden that you throw in the towel. Some people in business say that, as a broad generalisation, it is usually easier to deal with customers who are in business, as opposed to dealing with the general public. This stems largely from the fact that a percentage of the public are not businesslike in their dealings. If your dealings with the public consist only of supplying them with a pair of socks on your market stall on a Saturday, this will not greatly affect you; by contrast, listen to what many estate agents have to say about their dealings with Joe Public when it comes to handling the complexities of a transaction on the scale of purchasing and selling a house.

Bear in mind also the likelihood that the more complex and technical the product you are supplying, the more likely it is to throw up problems. A second-hand car is rather more likely to go wrong during the guarantee period, bringing a headache for the part-time motor dealer, than is a child's toy car supplied by a retailer of children's toys. If you have the expertise, remedying the defect in the computer, video, photocopier or other technically complex product you have supplied may not seem too great a problem; but bear in mind how aggravated customers can become if their complaint does not receive immediate attention.

If simplicity of operation is a prime objective of your small enterprise, reflect also that business life is less complicated if you deal in a standardised product, as opposed to a one-off product made specially for the customer. For example, a part-time business operating in London offers a choose-at-home carpet service, the customer making a selection from a range of sample books brought to the customer's home. Customer Mrs X chose a fitted carpet for her hall, stairs and landing. When she arrived home from work she was delighted to see that the fitter had made an excellent job of work, but was less than delighted to discover the carpet was not the colour ordered – the proprietor had made an error in completing his order form. The business was faced with the cost of removing the carpet. The proprietor estimated that to come across another customer with an identical hall, stairs and landing, and who wanted the particular carpet in that particular colour, would take fifty years: he opted to suffer the further loss of selling the carpet off as a remnant. The customer suffered the delay of waiting for her new carpet while the replacement was ordered from the factory and the proprietor incurred yet another loss: fitting costs for the replacement. During the period between fitting the original carpet and the fitting of its replacement, the customer rang the proprietor every other working day. Contrast this with the business dealing in a standardised product, of which it is able to hold stocks.

If, on getting it home, the customer's product does not work, this business can immediately supply the customer with an identical replacement and restore their good humour.

A decision that affects others

One other consideration before you launch off: do you have the support of your family? Not devoting your full-time attention to the business may mean you rely on the help of members of your family even more than usual. This will be especially so if, like many small businesses, your company headquarters is also your home: it will not help your business if your teenage daughter is impatient with customers on the telephone because they are blocking a call she is awaiting from her boyfriend. But one of the central messages of this book is that with sufficient thought the obstacles can be overcome: consider what they are likely to be before you meet them; then go round them or under them or over them. So, recognise that your plans are going to affect others: discuss your project with your partner and explain to your family why you are undertaking it. This can often avoid the problem coming up in the first place; but if not, if your teenager is going through a sulky period of adolescent non-cooperation, then arrange to install a second phone line and build the expense of that into your business costs.

> In your Personal Profile you set down WHEN you hoped to be in business: what might occur to cause this to be put off? Consider now how you could overcome these delaying matters.

CHAPTER THREE

Successful part-time businesses

In Chapter 2 we looked at some of the factors you should consider in weighing up whether a particular enterprise lends itself to part-time operations. It will help you in settling upon a suitable business idea to look at some businesses that are successfully run on a part-time basis. Perhaps one of these is something you could consider setting up; at the very least you can gain useful insight into the *sort* of enterprise that lends itself to fitting in with other things.

Party plan

Almost certainly party plan operations are more familiar to women than to men. The great majority of the products marketed in this way are directed at the female market; interestingly, even at parties where the product could be of interest to both sexes – for example, toys for sale to parents – almost invariably attendance seems to be 100 per cent female.

For the prospective small-scale entrepreneur the good news is that both start-up costs and operating costs in party plan are likely to be on the low side; for example, this method of doing business avoids the necessity for expensive High Street premises. This does mean, however, that there are many small players in the field as competition, but more good news is that many of these are amateurish operations.

If you are unfamiliar with how party plan works, the main characteristics are that sales are made at a gathering of people and the venue is someone's home rather than trade premises. The usual mode of operation is for the individual who does the selling – usually called a demonstrator – to recruit a hostess who then invites friends and acquaintances to the 'party'. The demonstrator presents the items for sale to the guests, giving them some background information about the company and its products. Or rather, this is what occurs with the larger, more professional operations; in practice, some of the one-person operations can be disappointing and boring for guests: the demonstrator, lacking the necessary outgoing personality, sets the goods out on display and stands by with arms folded.

Some party plan operations appear to be seasonal only, operating from the beginning of September to catch the Christmas trade; with toys, for example. Obviously, the disadvantage here is that this will not produce a regular income throughout the year; although, possibly, some operations are sufficiently successful in the hectic pre-Christmas period to produce income to cover a twelve-month period. Alternatively, such a seasonal operation could be combined with reaching customers at other times of the year via a different route, which brings us on to . . .

Shows and fairs

Throughout spring, summer and autumn up and down the country crowds flock to thousands of open air events: air displays, horse shows, steam rallies, county shows, dog shows, county fairs, agricultural shows, vintage car rallies and many more. While these different types of shows each have a particular focus, you will find at most shows an array of trade stands, many of whose wares are unconnected with the central theme of the event. The shows provide access to buyers without the need for retail premises.

Since the shows are held at times when the public can attend, this will suit you if you are running your mini-enterprise in addition to holding down a full-time day job. The same is true if you have a young family with no one else to look after them during the ordinary working week.

If you are going to operate your business by attending open air events you will have to adopt the farmer's philosophical attitude towards the weather. Be prepared to pack up your wares, travel long distances, set up your unit and your display – then see the crowds driven away by a downpour. You have to average your income over both good and bad days.

Shelter from the weather is one of the attractions of craft fairs which have so gained in popularity in the last few years. Again, if you are already occupied during the week, craft fairs have the attraction that many are held at weekends, especially Sundays. The 'cottage industry' image of crafts makes it seem a natural choice for part-time business, but the reality is that today crafts have become extremely competitive. Unless you have something very different, you will find lots of competition at a craft fair. But then, maybe you can come up with that Something Different.

Remember that not all product lines lend themselves to regular long-distance transportation; if, for example, you set up dealing in some kind of fragile ornament the care needed to pack up your wares for transporting to shows across the country may involve a disproportionate amount of time.

But the main drawback to reaching customers via fairs and shows is that your level of sales will depend upon there being a sufficient number of suitable shows within travelling distance; in this way you are limited in the volume of business you can achieve.

A different method of reaching customers, one with the ability to control how many selling days you have, is to run a business holding . . .

One-day sales

It is possible to create your own mini-event, to draw in your own crowd of potential customers, by staging 'grand, amazing, special' one-day sales.

Staging your own one-day sales as a means of reaching customers with your particular product has the advantage that, unlike the big, open air shows, the success of the event is not so dependent upon the weather.

Selling to customers in the home

If you need to fit your mini-business around a full-time job it could work very well if your customers need to see you at evenings and weekends. A business that involves visiting people at home – particularly one where you need to see both husband and wife – will almost certainly require a very high proportion of calls to be made outside normal working hours. Of course, depending on your product, a percentage of your customers may be retired and thus usually available during the day; but if you are yourself unable to make daytime calls during the working week you will find that most of these retired customers are happy to see you in the evenings or at weekends.

The sale of some products or services of necessity involves a call upon the customer's premises, most obviously where a price cannot be given to the customer without the supplier working out what is involved, for example a quote for the installation of a fitted kitchen. With some products there may also be an element of superior service in offering to call upon the customer at home, such as the choose-at-home curtain service that enables customers to select a fabric in the room in which the curtains are to be fitted, thus choosing from the different samples against the actual decor.

Some of the products commonly sold direct into the home may involve a business operation beyond a scale that would suit your part-time undertaking, for example supplying and fitting new kitchens – but is that beyond your capabilities if you do it with a partner? Or consider ways of scaling down what your business offers: in this example you could consider a mini-business that offers a service fitting kitchens customers have bought flat-pack from a discount warehouse.

Mail order

Mail order is the ultimate kitchen table business. The business opportunities columns of newspapers and journals have, for as long as I can remember, contained countless offers of books, courses and formulae telling us of the fortune to be made in mail order.

In the UK mail order is dominated by the operations of the household name companies who publish the telephone directory sized catalogues, in whose pages can be found everything from adaptors to word processors. But thousands of small mail-order businesses tell us of their existence through the pages of hobbyist and pastime magazines – from aero-modelling to woodworking. Some can be found in the pages of general interest magazines – especially women's journals – and among the thousands of advertisements in the pages of the bargain hunter's weekly resource, the *Exchange and Mart*. Pick up from your newsagent's display a journal catering for the estimated 2,000,000 stamp collectors: count up the advertisements and you may be surprised to discover 200 or even 300 mail-order enterprises, and perhaps half of these are businesses run in somebody's spare time.

Mail order is an example of a type of business that has its own golden rules which need to be observed if you are to have any chance of succeeding in the field. As with all business principles it is possible to point to outstanding enterprises which flourish in contravention of the norm, but be aware of the received wisdom in order to make an informed choice to disregard it. Setting aside the operations of the glossy mail-order catalogues, those running most small-scale postal businesses need to consider the following.

- You will have to consider postal/carriage costs: heavy or bulky items can be too costly to post.

- You will have to offer something that is not readily available locally to the prospective customer. Why should they go to the trouble of buying something through the post that they can buy in Woolworths?

- It may, however, be possible to persuade the customer to write out an order, find a stamp and walk down to the pillar box, if there is a sufficient price saving. Even hefty or expensive purchases such as hi-fi equipment and cameras are sold by mail order to bargain hunters.

If you will have to fit your mini-business around other major commitments, such as a full-time job or young children, mail order has the benefit that you don't have to run the shop in regular opening hours. Your orders will drop through the letter box and in all probability can wait to receive your attention at 9 p.m. when the children are in bed. (Bear in mind, however, that customers can become anxious within a few days of sending off their money.) And without the need for those expensive shop premises, it is very likely that you will be able to get into your new business with low start-up costs. Perhaps it is no wonder that so many of those advertisers in the business opportunities columns beckon you towards the enticements of a mail-order business...

Consultancies

Let us suppose that the offer on the next page appeared among the advertisements in the business opportunities column of your newspaper:

START YOUR OWN BUSINESS

* No big capital outlay!

* No stock required!

* No costly shop premises needed!

* No production costs!

* No expensive office premises – easily run from home!

* Big, big earnings within your grasp!

* THE IDEAL ONE-PERSON OPERATION!!

If all this sounds a little over the top, you will make the discovery if you write off for details of some of these opportunities that it is not unusual to receive a document couched in such terms, and with an equal number of enticing promises, if not more. If this style is not for you then be prepared to fill up your waste bin: it is surprising how many business start-up propositions use language more appropriate to an advertisement for a bingo club. Some of the material you receive will strain credibility, often because of its oversell as to how simple it all is. However, if our mock advertisement was to relate to the setting up of a business consultancy, it is possible that each of these claims would stand up to scrutiny.

So, what are the drawbacks that have been omitted by our fictional advertiser? The first hurdle to overcome is to light upon an area of expertise that you can offer. You will be looking for something to offer on a consultancy basis to business and/or public authorities. There may be something that leaps out immediately from your Personal Profile: perhaps you have a qualification or training, or job experience in some technical or scientific field. Or you may have some particular business expertise which could be marketed: perhaps you could market expertise in marketing? Perhaps you have acquired a skill picked up through an interest or hobby you have pursued?

Quite possibly you need to brush up or expand your expertise. Depending on how much lead time you can allow before you need to launch your operation, you may be able to acquire expertise via books or a course on the subject.

Some practitioners offer training alongside their consultancy services, partly because it may be easier to get a start as a trainer and to then build up contacts made through delegates attending training sessions. Getting yourself off the ground in a consultancy service is probably harder work than many other business start-ups. What you are offering is a classic example of an intangible product. The salesperson selling a Porsche can allure prospective customers with the depth of the shine in the bodywork; the prospect can feel the quality of the leather used for the upholstery. But the buyer of consultancy services cannot see the service until it is received and must place increased reliance on the description given to them. This element of greater trust applies generally to the selling of services and makes the salesperson's task more difficult. Training in sales techniques will overcome the problem and you can make a start on this in Chapter 12.

One possibility for finding someone who will give you your first commission is to approach former employers, assuming that you left them on reasonably good terms.

In settling upon a field of expertise to offer, a guiding principle to bear in mind is that your services must offer something for which the user will have intermittent or one-off need, rather than something which will be required all the time and which could therefore be fulfilled by an employee.

Do not confine yourself to considering the common services offered by freelance consultants: the more unusual

31

your field of expertise the more unlikely it is that the need is being met elsewhere. Perhaps you could set up as a consultant to people who would like to set up a part-time business?

If you have a full-time job, availability during the day could be a problem. It may not be insuperable, however, depending upon your terms of employment and how much time you wish to devote to your consultancy. For example, *Nick K*, who works in the planning department of a local authority, offers a consultancy service on planning matters to developers and others outside the area of his own employing authority. Nick's conditions of employment include flexi-time working, which enables him to accumulate hours and take an occasional day off in lieu. Like many professional people in employment and those working for big employers, he enjoys generous holiday entitlement, in his particular case six weeks. Nick is thus able to fit in some twenty working days over the course of the year for the purpose of visiting clients' premises.

Making-up services

Hopefully at this juncture in our review of other people's part-time businesses, you are beginning to be impressed with the number and diversity of possibilities open to you. If a consultancy service is not for you then let us turn our spotlight on to something completely different.

Some very tiny businesses – perhaps no more than pin-money operations – proclaim their existence to the world through the humble medium of the postcard on the newsagent's noticeboard. Scan a few of these boards and very likely you will find a simply worded advertisement for a making-up or alterations service, 'at reasonable prices'.

It may be curtains or loose covers, or dresses or suits. If you need to work from home and need flexibility in the hours you work you could join their ranks, if you have, or can acquire, the necessary skills. But perhaps your service could be a little more marketing orientated and a little more ambitious. Many customers only use a dressmaking service when in need of something for that all-important special occasion, of which the wedding dress is the most obvious example. An anonymous telephone number does little to encourage those for whom the ad is interesting, so include your name and a little detail about the quality of your services. Expect customers to approach you armed with their own fabric and pattern.

You could, of course, go beyond a mere making-up service, for example using your skills and equipment to manufacture clothes made to your own design – or, if you feel this aspect is beyond your capability, the design of a friend? Now you are no longer offering a service: now you have your own product to sell. Some sales could be made to friends and acquaintances reached by word of mouth or you could consider taking a stall in the local market one day a week. If you are going to be producing any sort of volume you will have to invest in an industrial sewing machine. Second-hand or refurbished equipment may prove no more expensive than a good-quality domestic machine bought new. Suppliers can be tracked down in the pages of the trade journal, *The Drapers Record*, as can wholesale suppliers of fabrics and trimmings; alternative sources for the latter are the general trade papers *The Trader*, published monthly, and *The Market Trader*, published weekly as a supplement to *The World's Fair*.

On the scale of business operations a making-up service is an example of a business at the smaller end; other possibilities for simple, income-producing activities include the following.

Secretarial/book-keeping services

When you set up your mini-business, you will need the telephone answering, typing carried out, photocopying facilities and the keeping of written records of account, among other things. What about, as a business idea, providing these support services to other small businesses? In setting up your own business you are part of a revolution, joining the swelling ranks of the millions of self-employed people. Many of these rely on the aid of family or friends to perform tasks they consider to be beyond their capabilities, or, more often, for which they have no taste; a small army of plumbers' wives spend their evenings converting a pile of invoices into a set of accounts. But not all plumbers' wives will knuckle down to these tasks. . .

Basic bookkeeping skills can be picked up in a couple of terms at evening class. You will need to advise your client to use the services of a qualified accountant as well, to deal with the Inland Revenue and Customs and Excise for VAT; your task is to prepare the written records which the accountant requires. Today, of course, many small businesses will use computerised accounting systems, which may well make it necessary for you to visit the client's premises to carry out the work.

Maintenance/repairs/servicing

We are all familiar with the advertisements in the classified columns of the local paper offering repair services for our washing machines, tumble driers and vacuum cleaners; possibly you have the skills to perform such services or the inclination to acquire the skills, but let your thoughts also wander over the possibility of offering a service in a less crowded market place. Domestic electrical appliances are examples of what, for most of us today, are essential items, but cast your mind over equipment or machinery used in pursuit of leisure activities. Could you service or repair power skis – sewing machines – electronic organs – swimming pools?

If you are tied down to the working day, five days a week, be prepared to pass up repair work that needs an immediate call-out, but many customers will be quite happy for routine servicing to be carried out at evenings or weekends. You may feel, however, that if you cannot give 100 per cent service to your customers you would do better to consider some other activity where your services would not fall short. On the other hand, an army of motorists struggle to keep their car on the road, who could not do so without the – albeit limited – services of the part-time mechanic.

Catering

Catering is a first thought for many people looking for a small business to set up: witness the recent boom in sandwich delivery services! But those small Japanese vans zipping round industrial estates unloading their trays of sandwiches demonstrate that it is possible to make a business out of supplying that which customers could probably quite easily provide for themselves. It is also an example of a product that is easy to manufacture and without the need for expensive production facilities. Yet not all sandwich-making operations remain cottage industries: one supplier to multiple outlets in East Anglia employs thirty staff on a production-line basis in a modern factory; a point at which to remind you that in selecting your business idea a consideration is whether you would be happy to confine yourself to a business that does *not* have real prospects of expansion into a full-time source of income or even beyond.

One word of warning: check out very early on with your local authority the complex legislation governing preparation and handling of foodstuffs – keep on co-operative terms with the people there!

Hire services

Almost certainly for a part-time business you will not wish to invest the capital necessary to enable you to offer the range of equipment and machinery offered by one of the generalist hire shops. But you could perhaps specialise in one particular type of machinery/equipment or confine yourself to items required for only one type of activity, e.g. gardening. Hiring out the unusual item, which is probably therefore in less demand, can lend itself well to a part-time operation.

If you will be operating from home the volume of traffic caused by callers at your premises could give rise to a need for planning permission. One way round this could be to offer a delivery service, although this might not be a practical proposition where your customer needs to see what is available and make their choice from a selection, such as fancy-dress hire. But if you are to operate a part-time business you must find inventive ways around the obstacles thrown up by this mode of operation: in this example perhaps customers could choose in advance from a book of pictures depicting the costumes and giving size details, and then make a booking for delivery on the date required.

Successful part-time businesses

The advantages of owning your own mini-business make it worth while turning yourself into a committee of ways and means!

Business History No. 1: *Terry W*

Field of Business: *One-day Sales*

Terry W's full-time job as a shift-worker left him only weekends in which to run a part-time business. Terry's main object was to accumulate savings to put down as a deposit on a house.

Terry enjoyed visiting markets; now instead of visiting them solely for pleasure his purpose was to observe and learn. He was struck by the number of 'punters' gathered round the 50p stall. There was no doubting the attraction of a bargain and no doubting that the one-price strategy appealed to the buying public.

Terry ordered a copy of the *The World's Fair*, a weekly journal which incorporates a section entitled *The Market Trader*. This is a source of supply for many of the lines found on markets. Terry had never visited a trade warehouse before and was apprehensive about how he would be received, and whether he should have a 'trade card'. Taking along a mate to bolster his courage he visited three cash-and-carry wholesalers in East London, each advertising a range of 50p lines. None of them asked if he was a trader or to see any proof of trading.

Hiring church halls, scout huts and similar accommodation, the sales were held on a Saturday in small towns and large villages. Advertising was mostly through the medium of door-to-door leaflets delivered locally a few days before the sale date.

Despite taking several hundred pounds at each of the first few sales, these takings produced only a small profit

37

that was not commensurate with the effort involved. Terry discovered that the majority of 50p lines could be bought from the wholesalers for around 30p + VAT, although some lines were considerably cheaper; a clearance or end of range line might be bought at a price which allowed him a threefold mark-up on cost. Terry needed to increase his takings: this he could do by either attracting more customers or by taking more money from the customers who came at present. Many of the venues used by Terry drew upon a limited local population, so that the first alternative was not viable. Terry's solution was to adhere to his principle of one price but to increase that price from 50p to £1.

In the course of time Terry made the pleasant discovery that some of the lines he had previously sold for 50p would also sell at £1!

CHAPTER FOUR

How to come up with other business ideas

Looking at other people's successful part-time businesses is just one approach you could take to finding a business idea for yourself: in this chapter you will find a range of other starting points you can use to generate business ideas. The methods set out are tried and tested: they have been used on numerous courses I have taught, during which a great number of ideas for new businesses have been generated. Many of the people on the courses used their ideas to start a successful business.

1. Drawing on your skills

Turn to the Personal Profile you completed in Chapter 1 and look again at question 4 where you thought about your skills.

A skill is an ability you have acquired, something you have learned to do, such as riding a bicycle. Office skills such as typing, or DIY skills such as carpentry or painting, could easily form the basis of a much-needed business.

Read through the list of skills you put down in question 4 of the Profile: now give this some fresh thought and add to the list skills you overlooked the first time. Do you have the skill of drawing? Writing skills? The skill of a photographer? Gardening? Hairdressing? Translating? Driving? A craft? Could you instruct others in any of these skills?

After that, look at question 5 on your natural abilities. A natural ability, unlike a skill, is a God-given gift, such as your talent for the 'gift of the gab'. Do any of these abilities suggest a business?

2. Making use of your experience

In question 6 of the Profile you set down the trades and occupations of which you have experience. Reading through this again you may well spot some omissions: for example, don't just include the paid work you have done but also put down any occasions on which you have helped out in the business of a relative or friend. Don't overlook temporary or voluntary work either.

Which of these could you make use of?

While considering what you know about, look at question 7 where you looked at your pastimes/hobbies. What interests you? In doing things you enjoy you may have picked up some saleable expertise upon which you could base a business.

3. Improving existing products and services

Setting up a service-based business is likely to be easier than one based upon a product, so we will look first at services.

WAYS TO IMPROVE SERVICES

One way to come up with an idea for a service business is this: as you use the services of others, ask yourself whether you could do what they are doing. When having that expensive washing machine repaired ask yourself whether you could set up a similar business. But unless there is a shortage of such services in your area, you will have to find a way to stand out and beat the existing competition. Could you acquire the necessary skills, for example at night school, and then could you offer a *better* service? Draw on your experiences as a customer: in what ways did the service fall short? We are all aware from our own experiences that many small businesses fall woefully short of offering a quality service. Don't be put off attempting a business offering a service just because others are already doing it – if you know from experience that what they are delivering can be improved upon.

IMPROVING A PRODUCT

Your Profile might suggest a product of which you have experience: drawing on that experience, could you improve that product? For example, perhaps now or in the past you have worked in sales: a good salesperson has to be well acquainted with their product and will be aware of its drawbacks. Perhaps you have worked on the production side and can use that insider knowledge. Have you had contact with customers, perhaps while working in an office, and learned while dealing with the customers what drawbacks the product suffered?

In trying to improve a product you can consider

● appearance;

● the product's function.

41

Could the product's appearance be made more appealing or attractive? Or can you improve the way in which this item works? You might be able to make it more convenient to use or more reliable or – today – more environmentally friendly. Can you make the product do more for the user by adding some new function?

How many products and services do you know that are perfect? Not many!

4. A new product

You do not have to be an inventor or a genius to come up with a new product. Most products new to the market simply represent a stage in an evolutionary process: most of them are not totally unlike anything that has gone before. It is not outside the bounds of possibility for your new little business with limited financial resources to create a new product – by modifying an existing one. What you do to the existing product must be such that you can then say you have turned it into something different, sufficiently distinctive for you to be able to claim that it is 'new'.

Most of the new products launched on to the market place by major companies will have involved large-scale investment, but it is perfectly possible for you to make something on a small scale if you have the necessary skills. It could be a new line in clothes that you can begin at least by making up at home. Many people assemble on a small scale simple, everyday products: it could be toys, an item of furniture or something ornamental. Small-scale production may in itself lead you to produce something that is sufficiently different from competing mass-produced items, to be so distinctive as to strike the customer as something new.

In most industries mass production entails uniformity. Small-scale production may enable you to individualise the items you produce. Going one stage further, you may be able to specialise in 'one-off' examples made to the customer's particular requirements. Of course, small-scale production and made-to-measure service almost certainly involves increased labour costs, thus resulting in a more expensive product, yet in most fields there will be a niche in the market for such a superior product.

Your Personal Profile may suggest a product that you could work upon to come up with an idea for a business. Here are more starting points for developing your thoughts.

- What about a luxury version of this product?

- Or a novelty version?

- Or perhaps a simpler version?

5. Filling a gap in the market

Buckingham Candy, a business set up in the late 1980s, supplies confectionery retailers with sweets – 'candy' – made in the USA. One of the co-founders of this successful business, **Juliana Goldenberg**, was reported as saying that the origin of the business was the idea of supplying something that was not already available. In this particular case it was a product that was available overseas but not in the UK. Asking yourself what is not available is a simple starting point that can be used in a number of contexts.

The complexities of importing are such that it is not for the faint-hearted and will probably be of interest only to those looking for a substantial part-time business. But export – import agencies will undertake the bulk of the work for you, charging a fee of course, such that you will have to import on a scale big enough to cover their costs. You can find out what exporters have to offer by writing to the overseas trade departments of embassies, asking for information on suppliers. Your local chamber of commerce will almost certainly have details of opportunities for members: this could be just one of the benefits you would get from a subscription. The business sections of most of the banks also regularly have listings of offers by overseas exporters.

Sift through your memories of holidays abroad: can you recall something that caught your eye and that you haven't seen in your own country? Have you travelled overseas as part of your job? Have you at some time or another brought back from abroad something to which you took a liking?

Coming closer to home, a useful and simple starting point for finding a gap in the market is to bring to mind items or services that you have not been able to obtain. Putting the same question to friends and acquaintances can often arouse a surprisingly vigorous account of their indignation at not being able to obtain supplies of X or somebody to do Y for them.

If this fails to elicit something promising, you could go on systematically to examine goods and services available in your area, to bring to light gaps in the provision of products and services. You will need:

● a comprehensive source to tell you what is available;

● a method for pin-pointing omissions from this.

A copy of 'good old *Yellow Pages*' will provide your first need. To deal with the second problem pick up a motoring atlas and leaf through it until you come across a geographical area which strikes you as having characteristics similar to your own. Consider such matters as the population size and whether it is an industrial or agricultural area. Then telephone directory sales at British Telecom – the number to ring is given in your own *Yellow Pages* – and order the edition of this wonderfully informative book for the area you have identified as similar to your own. Local newspapers can also be a valuable source of what is available, via their advertising. Scrutinise the entries in the yellow book and the advertisements in the papers: is a supplier in your area conspicuous by its absence? More likely, you will come up with a trade which has a smaller number of suppliers, which would still leave room for you to squeeze in.

This is a timely point at which to remind you to bear in mind while carrying out your researches that it is probably not worth your while reading through the section in *Yellow Pages* on dam builders: you are trying to come up with an idea suitable for a *part-time* business.

6. Meeting the needs of small markets

Little demand for a product means there is only a small market to serve – but a small market may enable a small business to survive, if only because there is insufficient demand to feed the appetite of the big boys who thus stay out of the field.

The size of a market may be shaped by any one of a number of factors; by turning these over in your mind you may come up with a product or service you are capable of delivering to such a market. The market may be small because:

- the business serves customers who have a specialist interest, for example, the supplier of foods for exotic pets such as reptiles;

- meeting a need for which there is only occasional demand, for example, hiring morning suits to wedding guests;

- the market has declined. Tastes change and yesteryear's mass market may have shrivelled to a rump of demand. This can be good news if it means the big players have withdrawn, leaving the existing market to be served by the small, individual business. Up to the 1950s a maker of equipment for horses featured in the list of the top 100 manufacturing companies!

7. Meeting new needs

That which today is commonplace and which we take for granted may not even have existed in the previous decade. The first man to walk on the moon would not have been able to watch a recording of it on his home video when he got back, but today the majority of people could do so. Social, economic and technological change may all bring in their wake new needs and desires that have to be met. Consider all those video machines that now have to be repaired.

What recent changes can you identify that have thrown up new opportunities for business?

Business History No. 2: *Liz S-L*

Field of Business: *Party Plan*

Liz's Profile had brought out how some ten years previously she had worked for a national party plan company retailing children's toys. On promotion to area manager, Liz had been responsible for recruiting demonstrators: she made the discovery that there was a scarcity of individuals with the right personality. With hindsight she also felt that the company's product line — children's toys — did not lend itself easily to making a special occasion of the parties for the guests attending; this was largely because the guests were not buying model police cars with wailing sirens for *themselves*. Customer self-interest in the product — and a resulting sense of anticipation and excitement — were absent.

An invitation to Liz's 'Hollywood-style jewellery party' promises glamour, items you don't see elsewhere, a glass of wine and of course some sparkle. Liz selects her stock with an eye on the ostentatious and the outrageous — to sell at above-average prices. She puts hard work into making her hostess's sitting room look different, the glamorous jewellery illuminated by a novelty spotlight in the guise of a movie camera — purchased from her local MFI store. A little originality and ingenuity goes a long way!

Liz points out that party plan is suited to someone who is not free during the day. This does not apply to her and she has experimented with a variation on party plan that appears to be gaining in popularity: the drop-in day party. This allows guests the freedom of calling in during the day at their convenience, perhaps after dropping off the children at school, or over lunchtime, or to meet friends and acquaintances for elevenses and a convivial cup of coffee.

Liz estimates that the total number of hours she puts in

during an average week amounts to some three days' work.

A slightly different slant is given to Liz's operations by promoting each party under the banner of a local fund-raising event or charity. For each party Liz asks the hostess if she has a favourite good cause to which she would like a percentage of the funds contributed. Wherever possible she makes this a local cause. The hostess is able to approach friends and acquaintances who are sympathetic to raising funds for the local playgroup, PTA, scouts, or animal sanctuary: 'Come and support us!' Now guests have two good reasons to attend a Hollywood-style jewellery party: to buy something nice for themselves and to feel virtuous while doing so.

CHAPTER FIVE

Off-the-shelf business opportunities

Taking up a pre-packaged business opportunity is likely to be a faster route into business than creating your own enterprise from scratch.

You may also like the support – sales meetings, advertising back-up, advice – that comes with some types of ready-made opportunities.

Or it may suit your temperament better to opt for something which others are already working successfully. And if you are new to business this could be a way of easing yourself in.

But there is a price to be paid for these attributes and it is not always to be paid in money.

What types of opportunity might you be offered? And in weighing up that type of proposition, what matters require particular attention?

1. Multi-level marketing (MLM)

The business opportunities section of *Exchange and Mart*

might carry 200 or more advertisements – a high proportion of these will prove to be MLM offers.

Also known as network marketing, MLM operations are now controlled by law following a number of earlier scandals. Without doubt, some participants have earned £££££s. The company's marketing literature is likely to trumpet fabulous sums earned by some fortunate individuals; almost certainly earnings have rested upon their ability to recruit others into the organisation. Naturally, there comes a point where the numbers already recruited are such that further recruitment becomes progressively more difficult and the earnings of those coming late to the scheme taper off.

A comparison of failed MLM operations with the runaway successes seems to indicate that not all products lend themselves to this method of marketing. Some companies turn to MLM in desperation with a product they have failed to launch successfully on to the market by more conventional means. But if the product itself is wrong and not a seller, MLM cannot magically turn it into a success. This method of reaching the customer seems to lend itself well to products which require some exposition or a demonstration. These functions the network marketer can perform, making a presentation of a product that in the store would languish on the shelf waiting for a customer to ask a sales assistant to explain. Products successfully sold in this way in recent years include perfumes, diet foods, security devices and water purifiers.

Typically, the organisation has a hierarchical structure, and the higher the level reached by a participant the greater the discount received off the retail price of the product. Huge numbers of hopeful people are recruited into MLM schemes – for an outlay usually no more than the price of a meal in a restaurant, they are 'in business'. The tiny financial risk is a big attraction. But in most MLM operations the likelihood is that most participants will fall by the wayside within a few weeks – like any other business opportunity its degree of success is related directly to the energy, skills and knowledge of the individual.

2. Agencies

Strictly speaking, in law an agent is a person who has the power to act on behalf of another and bind that other person. In the commercial world the term is often used loosely; what is offered to you as an 'agency' might in essence be more akin to a distributorship. The obligations incurred are very different.

If you are an agent the deals you make are between the customer and the person on whose behalf you are acting, called the principal. Where a sales agent makes a sale of the principal's goods the seller is the principal and it is the agent who has the obligations towards the customer, including the duties placed upon a seller by the provisions of consumer law.

With a distributorship properly called, the distributor is in essence a stockholder and the customer is the customer of the distributor. The contract of sale is between the distributor and the customer, and here the obligations of the seller are the obligations of the distributor.

A spot reading of the business opportunities columns of a Sunday newspaper reveals seven advertisements expressly seeking to recruit 'agents'; two other advertisers using less specific wording prove on enquiry to be also seeking what their literature describes as 'agents'. Four of the agencies are offers to act on behalf of finance brokers, generating applications for personal loans, second mortgages, re-mortgages and endowment mortgages. In all but one case the agent is to generate the business, from advertising and personal contacts. The one exception supplies 'leads' generated by advertisements placed in the agent's local press by the broker. (A 'lead' is a person who has demonstrated an interest as a prospective client, for example by completing and returning an enquiry coupon.)

Almost universally an agent's remuneration is in the form of commission on sales, the commission rate being lower where the principal supplies leads. As an agent you will incur some expenses which probably you are expected to cover from your commission: as a new agent you therefore take the risk of outlay on advertising and other expenses which will not be recouped if you are unable to attract sales.

Your start-up costs will probably include an agency fee: a sum payable on registration to cover the cost of the agency kit you will receive. The principal will view this as a demonstration of commitment by the applicant and the offer may include a refund of the fee when a stipulated number of sales has been concluded.

The terms of the agency agreement may be set out briefly in a letter of appointment, which is unlikely to cover all the points for consideration. A formal document comprising several clauses may indicate that the principal has greater experience of the use of agents and accordingly of the problems that can arise. Here are some points to consider.

- Will you be the sole agent for a given area? Or might you approach a prospective customer to discover that they have been canvassed by another agent?

- At what stage in the transaction does remuneration accrue? Is this when the order is placed or when the transaction is completed (which might be some considerable time later)?

- Is the commission lost in the event of cancellation by

the customer? What is the position where cancellation is due to the default of the company, e.g. late delivery, and unconnected with the agent's performance of their duties?

● Does the agent receive some remuneration where the agent generates an enquiry, e.g. a recommendation, outside their territory and which will be dealt with by another agent?

● Is the agent allowed to represent other principals?

This last point is vital where you intend to represent a number of companies in order to offer your customers a range of products. You may wish to act for a second manufacturer or importer, some of whose products complement those of the first principal, but some of which are in competition.

A source of agency opportunities is the British Agents Register, a professional association of sales agents. You will find the address in Appendix A. For the cost of the registration fee you will have access to regular offers of sales agencies. The association is for professional agents, but since many agents act for a number of principals most agency agreements will not envisage full-time represent-ation and you will be able to operate an agency as a part-time business.

3. Distributorships

You will recall that the vital distinction between an agent and a distributor is that where the sale is made by a distributor, in contrast to that made by an agent, the customer is the customer of the distributor, assuming the correct labels have been applied. Since commonly a distributor is in essence a stockholder, a further distinction is that a distributor can expect to make a capital investment in stock. My spot reading of the business opportunities column that turned up seven offers of agencies produced a higher number, nine, of offers to act as a distributor. For manufacturers or importers, marketing their goods through a network of distributors enables them to deal with far fewer entities (their distributors) rather than all the customers for their products. Distributors were sought for a range of natural beauty care products, energy control systems, burglar alarms, coin-operated telephones and a car-fuel saving device. The capital investment could be quite small, the minimum order for coin-operated telephones being three, an outlay of some £200.

Some of the considerations raised by agency agreements are also relevant to distributorships, including whether the distributor is to have an exclusive territory and whether the distributor is allowed to hold other distributorships. Consider also the following.

- Is there an obligation on the distributor to make a minimum purchase over a given period of time? Are you required, say, to purchase three units in each calendar month for so long as the distributorship agreement is in force?

- Does the supplier have an obligation to support the distributor with promotional material? Ditto advertising? The ability to run an effective advertising campaign may be circumscribed by a fragmented market for the product. The market for the pre-paid telephone included hotels and guesthouses, bedsits, nursing homes, retirement homes and restaurants, a scattered market to reach on a limited advertising budget. Such a problem in reaching the target markets may be a prime reason for the supplier opting for the distributorship route; individuals who will generate their own enquiries and sales locally, perhaps cold-calling on prospects.

- Does the supplier accept responsibility for defective goods, as between the supplier and the distributor? You will recall that since the sale is between the seller and the customer, the majority of the obligations under consumer law would fall upon the distributor as seller. The supplier is also a seller, under the contract between the supplier and the distributor, but since this is not a sale to a consumer the supplier may be able to exclude or limit liability.

4. Franchises

A franchise agreement permits you to use somebody else's business name and methods. By copying the proven methods of the franchisor (the party who grants the franchise) and trading under the banner of their established business name, the element of risk is slashed. But this assumes the franchisor has a track record for you to exploit. As a system of doing business franchising expanded rapidly in the 1980s and, jumping on the band wagon, some franchises were sold for new businesses that then failed to make the grade, taking the franchisees down with them. Franchising a new business has worked in a handful of cases where the company has been able to attract franchisees, not in the light of its track record, but on the basis of market research indicating the soundness of the business idea: clearly a less attractive proposition for a prospective franchisee than a business with an existing track record.

The overwhelming majority of franchise operations are for businesses operating five days a week (and more), and many of the well-known names require a capital investment beyond the realms of that which most of us would contemplate for a part-time business. The British Franchise Association will supply details of member companies offering franchises. These are listed in *Business Franchise*, a bi-monthly magazine available from newsagents. Probably the majority of these companies anticipate that the franchise would be operated full time. Not all franchisors belong to the Association and it is possible to turn up offers of a modest operation in the business opportunities columns of newspapers and journals. Do not expect the franchisor to be a household name, but you should expect evidence that successful franchisees are operating elsewhere and of the company's expertise of which you are to have the benefit.

Commonly a franchisor receives an initial payment with probably some recurring payment from then on, perhaps calculated as a percentage of turnover. With some operations there is no such 'royalty' payment after the initial franchise fee, the franchisor taking a 'cut' through a mark-up on the products supplied to the franchisee.

A spot reading of the 'Bus. Opps.' columns produced a will-writing franchise with a modest £250 as the initial franchise fee, and an interesting home improvement business giving kitchens a facelift in the form of new cupboard doors and work surfaces: franchise fee £400.

5. Business formulae

A high proportion of the advertisements under business opportunities are selling information. Very often this becomes apparent only from the reply you receive to your enquiry. The advertiser may be selling a business idea, which will be revealed to you on payment of a fee, or selling information on how to operate a particular type of business. You were forewarned in Chapter 3, if you have not previously responded to advertisements in these columns, to expect much of the literature you receive to make extravagant claims. It will be apparent – sadly – that many of these offers exploit the naïve and the gullible, and many are naked appeals to simple greed. The wording of an advertisement will often tell you what to expect.

'It's easy to make thousands every month!'
'Would you like unlimited income working three hours per week?'
'No selling, no administration, you just collect the profits.'
'Look! Look! No skills, no experience, no capital – just staggering profits!'
'The biggest money-spinner of all time – made me rich beyond my wildest dreams!'

All 100 per cent guaranteed genuine examples!

In among the hyperbole are some useful offers from those with experience and expertise of a particular trade, passed on through the medium of booklets or manuals. Most such blueprints can be purchased for only a few pounds. I have seen examples of such material – purchased in response to offers couched in sensible language – seemingly based on the author's first-hand experience, authoritatively written, revealing trade know-how such as margins, sources of supply, sales techniques and likely operational snags. A manual on party plan operations, for example, costing £20, was impressive in its detail and practical approach.

Among all the flotsam there is some information of value, but you will have to fish for it.

Sources of business opportunities

As we have seen, most newspapers carry a business opportunities column, although this may appear only once a week in the case of a daily newspaper. One or two of the 'quality' papers carry extensive advertising of this type, especially the Sunday editions. Journals which carry exclusively or mainly advertising material can be a useful source; reference has already been made to the hundreds of advertisements that appear in *Exchange and Mart*.

Trade magazines can be a particularly fruitful source of business opportunities. If you have not decided on a particular trade, draw up a list of, say, half a dozen trades in which you are interested or of which you have experience – refer back to your Profile – and for each trade place an order with your newsagent for the three most recent back copies of the relevant journal. Do not scan only the column headed business opportunities: pages of trade news, for example, may include an item about a manufacturer or importer seeking distributors. Especially do not confine your enquiries to offers of relationships such as agents, distributors and franchisees. The back-up and support offered by some manufacturers to those who buy their goods can clothe your business with an identity: an XYZ official stockist armed with display equipment, sales leaflets, catalogues, samples. Some suppliers will make suggestions and give guidance on methods for making sales. A manufacturer of natural cosmetics, with a range of more than 200 lines, offers 'start-up packages' comprising an assortment of the most popular products, together with sales aids such as sample testers and a booklet on how to sell natural cosmetics by party plan. Stationery and other items used in party plan operation, such as party invites, are also available from the supplier, and customers receive a regular newsletter of special promotions and ideas for increasing sales.

Off-the-shelf business opportunities

If you can find a product in which you have confidence and are happy to adopt, and which has back-up approaching this level, then you have found a business 'package' without either tying yourself down with some formal agreement or paying over a fee to buy the tie-up. I operated a part-time business in this way for over three years, a business that was sufficiently profitable and successful to be sold as a going concern. Not only had it given me an income but – although I did not know it at the time – my part-time business was building into a capital asset for the future.

Looking to the future of your business: in the longer term, is demand for your product/service likely to fall? If so, draw up now an outline plan of how you would react to falling sales. Consider, in particular, whether you would move into new products/services and, if so, what these might be.

Business History No. 3: *Cathy K*

Field of Business: *Jewellery*

In the same line as Liz S-L in Business History No. 2, jewellery, the small business run by Cathy K has developed its own product strategy to find a gap in the market.

Cathy began her business by simply selling anything within her price range offered by the fashion jewellery wholesalers she dealt with. She does no travelling to buy her stock, ordering by post from wholesalers' and importers' lists. Living in a rural area, and with a need only to generate a small income, Cathy set up stall at local village fêtes, carnivals, fun days and similar events. An absence of competition, and the glittering jewellery, created interest.

Because of the need to protect her trinkets from inclement weather, Cathy invested in a walk-in type of market stall. This type of unit commonly utilises a framework made of heavyweight steel to enable it to withstand high winds — Cathy's muscles soon began to ache! Cathy was also to make the discovery that to set up the unit on her own and then make an attractive display of her stock took almost three hours. For a show with opening hours from 10.00 a.m. until 6.00 p.m. Cathy was spending twelve hours on site, plus travelling and loading/unloading times at either end of the day. Her profits needed to increase!

Cathy's strategy was to specialise: to aim a particular type of fashion jewellery at a particular segment of the market. Thus were born her *Jewellery Pets*: earrings, brooches, bangles and any other item of jewellery depicting living things other than humans. Now at gymkhanas, dog shows and open days at animal sanctuaries, the crowds are delighted to take home tortoises, parrots, butterflies, lizards, dogs of every description, horses, cats, bats and spiders, in gold or silver plate, painted wood or enamel.

Since purchases of fashion jewellery are occasional only, and usually of small value, mark-ups in the trade have to be high: the strong appeal of Cathy's menagerie to animal lovers enables her to work on even higher margins.

PART TWO

DOING IT!

> **THAT'S IT!**
> You've decided!
> You are going to set up doing this:
> (*set down your business idea here in a few words*)

Once the firm decision is made – at last – your reactions are probably a mixture of relief at having resolved what you are going to do and excited anticipation at the prospect. It is going to be interesting – and a challenge – *and* it is going to bring in some money...

Shall we go out to celebrate?

It's a shame that your mother is coming to stay for a few days, starting tomorrow. You'll have to put off getting started on your business until next week. It's a pity, but it can't be helped. And then it's starting to get close to Christmas and there'll be all that to do... Perhaps it would be better to leave it till the New Year.

Or perhaps you'll be going on holiday soon and you will have to leave things until after you get back from your trip. Or perhaps you want to get the new extension for the house out of the way first. Or perhaps you ought to wait until you haven't so much to do at work.

What a pity. You have just joined the millions of people who will *not* start their own business.

It is all too easy to put off your new venture.

A recent survey revealed that some 60 per cent of people would like to have their own business. Huge numbers of these go through the process of seeking out a business idea and reach the stage of fixing upon what their business shall be. But they never leap off.

Perhaps it is because they are afraid of failure or because they lack self-confidence. With others, it is through lack of business experience, while some feel their friends and family will laugh at them.

Nearly all of them regret that they never gave it a try.

To get *you* started here is a SIX-DAY ACTION PLAN.

Here are six useful relevant activities that will get the wheels turning. Resolve to work your way through these activities and at the end of Day Six you will have momentum, and you will be well into the groundwork for your own part-time business.

Six-day action plan

Mindful that you are launching a part-time business, it is for you to decide how much time you can allocate to a task on any particular day. But even half an hour would at least get that task under way...

Day one

> Analyse how well your competitors meet the customer's needs and desires. Rate each main competitor for product features, range, service, availability, price.

Make a start on your **market research** (MR). Don't be put off by that term. It is frightening how, in my experience, people running small businesses carry out negligible market research. Ask them about their market research and many of them grimace. It is staggering that people will set up a business *solely* on the basis of a hunch. And then run the business without the benefit of MR to:

1   help ensure its continued survival;

2   improve its profitability.

Intuition may have been the mother of your idea, but thereafter you can make use of something more tangible to minimise your risk. Big business uses it: successful, household name companies spend a fortune on it. Products are given life thanks to market research. Probably you are thinking you do not have the resources of Cadbury's or Ford. So photocopy the following notice, enlarge it to fill a sheet of A4 copying paper and pin it on the wall above your desk.

MARKET RESEARCH

1. My business can carry out simple exercises in MR. It will gain enormous, disproportionate benefit.

2. Information available to and used by Famous Name Multi-Million PLC is available to me. At minimal cost. Or even free.

I have discovered that the word 'research' deters many small-scale entrepreneurs. Essentially, market research is about finding out what you can about who is, or might be, a customer for your product, and what alternatives they could buy from somebody else.

This does not have to be a major project, costly, using market research companies. Learn about your competitor's product by reading their advertisements. Obtain a copy of their sales leaflet, buy or borrow their product, talk to somebody who has bought and used it. Pose as a prospective customer, or arrange with a friend to do so, to hear your competitor's sales pitch.

Pre-launch, you are wondering whether your product will work in this area/at this time/at this price/at all. Go out and question prospective customers. Devise a simple questionnaire. You want to know the following.

- Do you buy widgets now and, if not, why not?

- Who do you buy from?

- How much do you pay?

- How often do you buy one?

- What don't you like about the widgets you buy now?

- Would you pay more for X improvement?

- How much more would you pay for this improvement?

- Would you buy bodgets if they were available?

- How much would you pay for bodgets?

> **Analyse why your product or service will be AT LEAST as good as the competition**

Go out with your questionnaire and ask the people in the high street for a minute or two of their time, just like the professional market researchers and opinion pollsters. If your product is not aimed at the general public – for example, you aim to supply schools – you can telephone your interviewees or visit their premises.

'We're carrying out market research', is a lie not infrequently used by salespeople to get a foot in the door, so expect the occasional interviewee to misinterpret your motive and brush you off.

Guidelines used by professionals in devising a questionnaire:

- avoid leading questions (questions which suggest an answer);

- avoid vagueness, e.g. 'Do you eat doughnuts *sometimes?*';

- avoid complex questions;

- avoid unfamiliar words in your questions;

- avoid questions where one answer may confer status on the person answering, e.g. 'Do you view programmes aimed at intelligent viewers?';

- avoid questions that are too taxing on the memory.

Here you are carrying out your own original market research. In addition to this, research, study and analysis already carried out by others is available to you. Market research companies, universities, trade associations and other bodies, produce reports and studies on individual trades and sectors of a trade. This is valuable information: you could pay hundreds of £s for a copy of a report based on extensive professional research, which is probably not an outlay your part-time business can afford to make. One route to learning about your trade and its markets is the business library of the nearest university, of which the UK now has some ninety, including the former polytechnics. Most universities have business schools with specialised libraries and many make their services available to the local community. Expect to pay some fee for this facility, but it will allow you to tap into the inter-library service. The report or study you want is held in a library somewhere and can wing its way on loan to the library you are using. If the library does not make its services available to non-students, access to its facilities could be another reason for you to enrol on a short course or part-time course on business start-up or some other aspect of business.

Useful basic information may be found near to hand in the reference and business sections of your local public library.

A further source of access to information is the high street banks. All the major banks appear keen to win the small business account and offer a range of ancillary services to woo customers. In some cases this includes a free information service providing data on markets, trends, buyers and other background information on your particular trade.

Flushed with enthusiasm for your business idea, you may feel other tasks are more urgent – or pleasurable – or that you could be generating revenue instead of reading up 'research' in a library. Remember that time and money that goes on market research can save time and money. If you attack the market on too many fronts you are in danger of spreading your resources too thinly: chasing after X potential buyer when Y potential buyer is a better bet. Look for the differences between potential buyers, differences that would influence their decision to buy. Differences such as age group, income level, social class, occupation type. Then ask who is more likely to buy. Direct your efforts at *them*, rather than spread your efforts too thinly. Marketing professionals call this 'segmenting the market'.

As soon as you have your first customers you have your own unique source of market information. **Your business cannot stand still.** Because you are making sales, because you are making a profit, doesn't mean you will survive. If you do not

- improve your product;

- find new markets and

- devise new products,

your competitors will. This is one of the lessons the conquering Japenese have so impressed upon UK business. So talk to your customers. You want to know what they liked about your product (so you can retain it – perhaps), what they didn't like (so you can change it, for sure), what they felt was missing, what other products they would be interested in.

On my business training courses we give each participant a questionnaire to complete at the end of the course. Time and again participants on our Be Your Own Boss short course revealed through these that although they now had the skills and knowledge to run a business they did not have a business to run: because they did not have a business idea. These replies prompted us to devise our most successful product, the short course 'How to Come up With an Idea For a Business'. Thank you market research.

Questioning our clients enabled us to spot a gap in the market and fill it. An example of performing the classic marketing function: ascertaining the needs of the market and then fulfilling those needs.

Researching the market: an example of how part-time need not equate with amateurish.

A QUESTION OF PRICE

Your market research will help determine the price you set for your product or service. Get this wrong and you won't make any profit. Yet it is another area where newcomers to business so often take a simplistic, uninformed approach. They work out their costs, then add to this some arbitrary percentage.

The only price you can charge is the price customers will pay. This may be the same as the price calculated by the cost plus formulation, or it may be less, or it may be more. What the customer will pay you is hugely influenced by what they could pay others.

> Compile a listing of the prices charged by your main competitors for the product or service you will be offering.

Where do you intend to position yourself in the market place? This is a major factor in arriving at a price. Are you, for example, targeting upmarket, offering high quality or exclusivity? For most buyers, price is an indication of quality and can be particularly influential on the customer's mind where it is difficult to assess quality.

A popular misconception among newcomers to business – and those who are not in business – is that to succeed in business all that has to be done is to price your product below the price which customers now have to pay. But does a bargain price fit in with where you wish to position yourself in the market? With the image you wish to create? Value for money pricing is but one strategy open to you, one way of winning customers. Instead, perhaps your product or service could offer customers some additional feature not available from the competition, and in this way you distinguish yourself from competitors and edge into the market place while your customers pay the same price. Or perhaps, for the additional benefit, they are willing to pay a higher price?

And are you sure that you can afford to sell it cheaper than everybody else? Quite possibly as a part-time operation you are in a position to work on smaller margins or perhaps your overheads are lower – but then again as a small operation some of your costs may be higher, for example you may not get the benefit of quantity discounts.

You may also need to acclimatise yourself to the high margins which are the necessary practice of some trades. The uninformed lay person may be scandalised by mark-ups of, say, 400% on costume jewellery. This is an example of a trade where volume of sales is low: a pair of fashion earrings is a product bought only periodically by most customers – if you are selling something to the same customer every week, a regular repeat purchase such as a can of beans, you can afford to work on tighter margins. Observe also that it is easier for customers to make price comparisons if they buy the same item regularly, which acts as a constraint on your pricing. And then the customer who only buys an item occasionally is likely to be less inhibited about price – e.g. a gift as an anniversary present – than if they have to make the outlay repeatedly, such as petrol for the car.

The price is a big factor in the decision to buy: most customers have limited funds for their purchase. The higher the price the smaller is the number of potential customers. Of special relevance to you, running a part-time business, is the volume of sales you want – and can handle. Higher prices usually equals smaller turnover, and this may suit you.

THE PRICING OF SERVICES

With the pricing of services you have to face this particular problem: the tendency for customers to look only at the number of hours expended by the person providing the service and to base their reaction to price on that. You will have heard someone say, 'I was only with my solicitor half an hour and he charged me £30!' Indeed, such may have been your own reaction in the past to your solicitor's bill. If your business is to be the provision of a service, now you face the problem of clients who overlook the overheads behind the scenes: the phone, the electric, the rent, business rates, the secretary's wage, the secretary's national insurance, etc., etc., etc. Hopefully, with a scaled-down operation your costs will be similarly scaled down, but you can't escape overheads altogether.

Then, as the provider of a service, you will also come up against the perceived 'value' placed upon your service by customers in the market place. Look at the value we all place upon the services of a doctor who is able to make us well again – hence the fees generated by consultants in private practice! But will your service enjoy such perceived value?

The still higher fees levied by the Harley Street consultant give us a clue to one of the ways in which you may enhance your fee rate: status. What will enhance the status of your business will depend in general upon the nature of the service you provide, although what confers status in the eyes of one person may not impress another. Formal qualifications will almost certainly enable you to put up your prices. The value of these in the eyes of the customer is not always appreciated by the tradesperson who provides a service. If you are a qualified electrician, make this known in your advertising, sales literature and business cards: this will give customers increased confidence in their ability to rely on you. In many types of service it is not technically feasible for the customer to verify whether the service has been properly provided: formal evidence of an apprenticeship served will facilitate the customer placing their trust in you – for this element of security they must expect to pay a higher rate.

Membership of a professional or trade association confers status. For example, it may be that the service you provide is of such a type it renders your business eligible for membership of the Guild of Mastercraftsmen. Membership of such an association is intended to reassure potential clients of minimum standards. Joining this or other similar organisations may not be as difficult as you might expect: you will be required to provide evidence from customers of satisfactory standards of work, but this is something you should be able to achieve after only a short period in business. Membership of the Guild or a similar body will

73

usually entitle you to display an impressive logo in your advertising and sales literature, all of which should help to fatten your prices.

Simply getting yourself known will help you to pump up the fees for your services: it is remarkable how your bill will be more digestible to some clients if they have recently heard you on the radio, or seen your picture in the local paper. It is easier to become something of a personality than you may think and we look at ways of getting you a degree of fame in Chapter 13.

The services of a doctor provide us with a further clue as to how you may bolster your prices. We will swallow the enormous bill of the private consultant who has cured us of our illness: we have derived from the consultant's services an overwhelming life benefit of good health. So another approach to the pricing of services is to look at the benefit your service confers upon the client. Just as many customers weigh the price they expect to pay in terms of the hours provided, so too many newcomers to business define their pricing policy by fixing a rate per hour which will provide a reasonable return; to arrive at their bill they simply multiply the rate per hour by the hours expended. Yet for some small effort in terms of time your customer may receive major benefit from your service. It is open to you to take the view that the price paid should reflect the value of what the customer has received. Let us suppose you operate a debt-collecting service. Your client has been unable to recover £500 due to him. You send out a letter produced on your wordprocessor: the debtor does not like a debt-collecting agency on his tail, and remits a cheque for the full amount. Your costs, including a few minutes' labour, are minimal but the client has received £500 benefit. Are you really going to bill him for ten minutes' work?

The inherent problems in the pricing of services are an example of the distinctions between providing a tangible physical product and providing a service. It is a reminder too of this distinction: as a generalisation, your earning power over a given number of hours is probably potentially greater in a product-based business than a service-based business. Of course, your ability to earn in a set number of hours from the provision of services must depend upon the level of fees which you can charge for those services. But if, say, your service is one which does not require either qualifications or the employment of great skills – or you face intense competition – it may be that your earnings' limit is something quite modest. Perhaps in the same number of hours you could have delivered a number of products, each of which provided you with a profit. There are only so many hours in the week – particularly for the part-time business – and in a service-based business if you are the service provider there is a physical limitation upon your earning capacity – unless of course you are to expand by employing others to provide the service also. If so, perhaps then for you it would be more accurate to say that as a generalisation it is probably easier to make money *faster* in products than in services: it is easier and quicker to purchase an extra 1,000 widgets from your wholesaler than to find, recruit, train and supervise personnel.

Whether you are in products or services, consider ways of bolting-on value to what it is you supply, of providing something extra. It may be that you can add, say, 10 per cent to the market price of what you are selling at a cost to you of 2.5 per cent. Consider, for example, how packaging can inflate the value of the product, such as with the packaging of perfumes. If you are offering a service, consider adding on a guarantee: at your sales presentation show the potential customer your guarantee certificate, beautifully printed in fancy type – surely a service that comes with such a guarantee is worth more than one with no guarantee?

Day two

Make a start on your **business plan**.

The expression 'business plan' is commonly used in business to denote a written document. If putting things down on paper is not your favourite task, rest assured that the job need not be a daunting one.

You will find devising your business plan a really useful exercise.

If you will be borrowing money from your bank for start-up costs, unless the sum involved is very small indeed, the bank will almost certainly want to have sight of your plan.

Much of this plan is already in your head or perhaps in some notes you have already made. If your needs will be met by a very small spare-time operation whose aim is to produce some useful pin money, devising a short, simple business plan will help ensure you have given consideration to the important matters to which attention must be directed in even the simplest of business operations. It may be that you need a document no more than three or four pages in length. If your business will be a substantial undertaking, perhaps involving partners, or sizeable start-up costs, or one incurring potentially onerous obligations, your plan may amount to a document of a score or more pages.

Here is an easy way to produce your business plan: in their eagerness to attract business accounts, most of the high street banks produce literature to help the customer who is setting up or running a small business. This free literature usually includes a booklet divided into sections in which the customer sets down the relevant details to produce, in almost painless fashion, a business plan.

Matters covered in a business plan usually include:

- a biographical note detailing the background and experiences of the proprietor, partners or directors as the case may be;

76

- the nature of the business;

- start-up costs;

- market research carried out;

- projections of income, outgoings and profits over a given period;

- sources of finance;

- premises required;

- short, medium and long-term plans.

The need to set out this last item will direct your mind to where you want your business to take you: better to think this through now rather than to lurch into a crisis when the business is in motion and the running of the business diminishes your thinking time. What if – joyously – your product or service is stunningly successful and the orders pour in? *Is* this joyous? Do you really want to expand? Do you want to take on staff or more staff? Do you want the time spent on your business to eat into the time devoted to other activities? If you are tempted to react, 'I'll cross that bridge if I ever come to it', bear this point in mind: a runaway success may be out of control. Many people who are novices to business are surprised to discover that a business with overflowing order books can suffer as many problems as a business with too few customers. If you cannot cope with the volume of work and cannot meet orders, your customers will cancel: in an overheated business, orders melt away. If you cannot maintain your quality control, the hours can be eaten up by the time devoted to correcting faulty products and dealing with complaints. Truly, a business can be the victim of its own success. So how big do you want your little business to grow? Be clear in your own mind at which stage you would wish to pull on the brakes.

It may well be that your business plans justify the costs incurred in seeking the help of an accountant in devising your plan and, in particular, some assistance with the financial aspects.

Day three

Check out whether you need a **licence** for your new business. If you have not run your own business before you may be surprised to learn that as a general rule you will not need to apply for a licence to set up in business. In our free enterprise society the basic principle is that any person is free to set up and operate a lawful business without the consent of HM government. This basic freedom is, however, subject to these considerations.

1. This absence of a general licensing requirement is subject to a number of exceptions governing particular trades. For example, if you wish to operate as a bookmaker, or retail alcohol, you will need a licence.

2. You may require a licence to operate your business in a particular manner, for example, if you will be making door-to-door sales.

3. You may find that while your business is not required to be licensed, one or more of your business *activities* is subject to some form of licensing. For example, while you do not need a licence to set up retailing lawnmovers, if you sell these to consumers on credit,

for this you will need to be licensed under the Consumer Credit Act.

4. You may discover that your local council has its own licensing requirements for a particular trade operating in its locality. A local authority has power to make by-laws governing its area and some authorities use these to regulate business activities.

Bear in mind also that to operate in certain trades or professions, even part time, there may be a legal requirement for you to possess a particular qualification or to belong to some regulatory body. Most trades have a professional association, open to members of that trade, and in practice you may find that although there is no legal requirement to belong to the association, your business will be hampered if you trade as a non-member. An example is the security industry: here, at present, companies installing burglar alarm systems are not required by law to join the industry's professional association. In practice, however, where an insurance company requires the insured to install an alarm, almost certainly the insurer will only recognise an installation by a company which is a member of the professional association.

Ascertain your licensing position from your local authority's trading standards department or from the sources of information listed in Chapter 6.

Newcomers to business often confuse licence considerations with the question of planning permission. Planning permission is concerned with the use to which you put premises and is a separate matter. If you set up a part-time business servicing sewing machines you probably do not need to apply for any sort of licence to offer such a service to the public, but if you were to operate your business from home it could be that you would need to apply to the local authority for planning permission to use your home for such purpose. Planning permission is looked at in greater detail in Chapter 8.

Day four

Make a start on matters connected with the important question of the **form** your business is to take. Will you operate as a sole trader, a partnership or a registered company?

Each has its respective advantages and drawbacks; these need weighing up in the light of your personal strengths and weaknesses, and the individual circumstances of your particular business, including the scale of your planned operations.

THE SOLE TRADER

Of the different forms your business can adopt, this is the simplest to set up. Unlike a company, you are not required to comply with a registration requirement. Unlike a partnership, control is solely in your hands and, thus, so too are the profits.

On the minus side of the balance sheet, you are personally liable for the debts incurred by your business. Often this is not understood by those who run a small business. **Jason** is a part-time self-employed mobile mechanic, operating as a sole trader. He uses the business name **Relyonme Mechnical Services**. When the business has been established for some months, Jason comes to regard the business as a separate entity from himself; in speech he refers to 'the business' and has been heard to say, 'the business owes me money'. But in the eyes of the law Jason is the business, and the assets and debts of the business are assets and debts of Jason. If your business could conceivably be running up sizeable debts, bear in mind this point: the sole trader is liable for the debts of their business to the full extent of their personal assets. If you were unable to meet the liabilities and your creditor insituted legal proceedings, the bailiff could enter your home and carry off saleable property.

THE PARTNERSHIP

We have raised earlier the question of whether you should consider sharing the joys and burdens of running your business in tandem with another. In addition to a partner bringing skills and experience to complement your own, you also get another pair of shoulders to carry the responsibilities that go with business ownership. It is someone with whom you can pull up a chair to talk things over.

One of the matters any prospective partners have to consider is how much time each partner will be expected to devote to the business. Where the partners are not in the straightforward situation of each giving their full-time attention, careful consideration must be given to the degree of input expected and to the extent to which the partners will need – and be able – to come together.

The commitment of each partner is but one of the matters which needs to be covered by the partnership agreement. This is the formal document which sets out important aspects of the relationship between the partners. Devising such an agreement will focus your attention on a range of matters which need to be considered by those entering upon a partnership.

Almost certainly you will need professional help in devising your agreement: the sums expended now on solicitors' fees could represent a considerable saving on the legal fees you could expend in the future on a dispute created out of a vague or incomplete partnership agreement. All too often the first occasion on which a solicitor is consulted on a partnership matter is when relations are breaking down. The client asks, 'What I want to know is, can my partner do this?' The solicitor replies, 'The answer to that is simple: what does it say in your partnership agreement?' Back comes the response, 'We didn't put anything in writing. . .'.

Setting aside the common reluctance to expend money on solicitors' fees, one explanation for this phenomenon is that the partner who is minded to suggest drawing up a formal agreement feels this might be interpreted as showing lack of trust in the word of the partner. This factor looms especially large where the partners are related: 'I didn't want it to look as if I didn't trust my wife's brother'. Overcome your reluctance: explain to your partner that it is not a question of trust, but simply good business practice. It will give certainty to matters. It is a breeding ground for disputes and resentment if, for example, a partner is unclear as to the extent of the time commitment they are expected to make to the business.

The desirability of not entering casually into a business partnership over a drink with a friend in a pub may be underlined by this apparently little-known principle of law: a partner, like a sole trader, is liable for the debts that partner incurs on behalf of the business – but in addition the partner is also liable for debts so incurred by his or her partners. No doubt in drawing up the agreement your solicitor will advise you that it is possible to insert a clause restricting the authority of a partner to incur debts on behalf of the business. This does not afford complete protection to the other partners: they may remain liable for obligations incurred on behalf of the business, despite the partner exceeding his or her authority in entering into a particular transaction. This possibility arises because the law feels the need to protect individuals who enter into transactions with business partnerships and who, as outsiders, cannot know of the restrictions placed upon the authority of a partner by an agreement made with the partner's colleagues. Thus, if a partner enters into a transaction of a type which outsiders could reasonably expect the partner to be empowered to make, the other partners will be liable for the debt incurred. If a partner so acts beyond his or her authority, that partner will be in breach of the partnership agreement, and the other partners may then sue for breach of contract, but they will remain liable on the debt themselves, even if they are unsuccessful in recovering money from their errant partner.

An agreement will set out the rights and responsibilities of the parties, and provide for eventualities. The more important matters for which it might make provision include:

● provision of capital;

● division of profits;

● powers of the partners (e.g. to make contracts);

● drawing of cheques;

● how the partnership is terminated;

● procedure for dealing with disputes;

● drawing money from the partnership;

● time to be devoted to partnership affairs;

● arrangements for property brought in by partners.

Should you decide a partnership is for you, your solicitor

will advise you in detail on the contents of your agreement.

But if you wish to run your business with others, you have also the option of forming a company.

THE REGISTERED COMPANY

In the eyes of the law a company is a person, the law recognising two types of persons: human beings and companies. When you have completed the procedures laid down for company formation, your company will be born: an official, the Registrar of Companies, issues a certificate of incorporation, rather like a birth certificate, giving the date on which the company was incorporated – your company's birth date. Just as a human being will be given a name, so too must the newly arrived company.

A lawyer uses the term 'company' in the sense that we use it here, to denote a company which has been brought into existence by following the procedures laid down for registration. Confusingly, in the world of business, the expression is sometimes used by non-lawyers to denote a partnership. Indeed, some partnerships adopt the word as part of their business name, as in 'Smith & Co.'. This confusion is regrettable, since a company in the lawyers' sense is a very different animal from the partnership. A registered company has in the eyes of the law an existence, an identity, distinct from that of the persons involved in the company. A number of consequences flow from this principle, the most important of which concerns the legal liability of what are called the members of the company. The overwhelming majority of registered companies are limited companies: this is where the liability of the members of the company for the debts of that company are, unlike partners, limited.

If you are unfamiliar with companies, to understand who is a member we need to look at the purpose of companies. Two major purposes can be singled out: first our economic system wishes to encourage people to invest in business; the limited company is a vehicle by which individuals can invest without running the risk of exposing themselves to untold losses, without taking liability beyond the investment they put in. Secondly, the company is a means of bringing together those who have the desire and expertise to run a business – such as you – and those that have funds to invest in business, but do not wish to involve themselves in business operations. Those who put up the money are the members of the company, in the commercial world more usually called the shareholders, and those who manage the affairs of the company are the directors. A person may be both a director and a shareholder, and in practice directors will usually hold shares in their company.

The capital of the company is divided into shares, for example £500 capital divided up into 500 shares of £1 each. The liability of a shareholder in a limited company extends only to the value of his shares. Thus if the shareholder has 200 £1 shares, the limit of his liability is £200. In this way, Auntie Vi can invest in your new venture without worrying that she is risking her life savings.

For the individual who wishes to invest in a business without running the risk of unlimited liability, the registered company is the usual vehicle, but it is also possible for a member of a partnership to enjoy a similar limitation of liability. However, such limitation of liability is not open to all the partners, as it is with all the members of a company. Further, unlike the ordinary partners, a partner with limited liability cannot take part in the management of the business. In practice these complications ensure that limited partnerships are not common.

On learning for the first time of the concept of limited liability, the reaction of some prospective entrepreneurs is, 'What is to stop me setting up a limited company, running up a lot of bills, enjoying the proceeds, then sitting back with my arms folded while the creditors whistle for their money?' The law is not such an ass! The concept of limited liability is swept aside in the case of those who use the company for fraudulent purposes; nor does the law permit company directors recklessly to run up bills and incur obligations. Broadly speaking, the directors must take care to minimise losses once they should have realised the company would go under.

So far as the law is concerned it is not possible to have a one-person company: the legal requirement is for a company to have at least one director and one company secretary. Although a director can also act as company secretary, a sole director cannot do so; therefore if a company is to have only one director, a second person must take on the role of secretary. The secretary is the chief administrative officer of the company. It is thus possible for one person to have sole management of the business affairs of the company, if some other person will act as secretary. The function of secretary could be performed by your accountant, who will, of course, charge you an accountant's fee for the work performed in this capacity. Some company registration services (explained in more detail below) will act as company secretary, carrying out the duties prescribed by law, usually in return for a fixed annual fee. The duties placed by law upon the secretary include such matters as lodging the annual accounts with the Registrar of Companies.

The protection of limited liability has great appeal for new businesses – but there is a price to be paid. If you opt for the allure of limited liability, expect the 'bill' you pick up to include:

- the costs of forming the company;

- higher accountancy costs involved in auditing (verifying) the accounts of the business;

- loss of privacy – the documents you are required to file with Companies House are open to public inspection, including your accounts;

- the operations of a company are subject to much greater regulation than the affairs of a partnership or sole trader;

- the administration burden is much greater – the company is required, for example, to keep various registers.

Complications flow from the principle that a company is a person in the eyes of the law. One at least of these can have an immediate practical impact on your pocket. A sole trader will be required to account annually to the Inland Revenue for the profits of the business; in the interim the trader may be making drawings for him or herself from money coming into the business. By contrast, if you elect to carry on your business through the medium of a company and take up the role of director, money coming into the business belongs to the company. If the company pays money to you in your capacity as director for work you do for the company, then the company is required to operate PAYE as would an employer. Thus your company must operate the pay as you earn machinery and you, on the receiving end, will suffer tax when the payment is made.

Whether or not you should operate through a company is a difficult question: if you opt not to do so at this stage, it is open to you to review the possibility in the future if you find your business, together with your obligations and liabilities, has grown.

Setting up the company
Giving birth to a company can be a fairly painless process. The procedure can be completed for you by a company

registration service. Expect this process to take some weeks. Or you can buy an 'off-the-shelf' company: a ready-made company which the registration service guarantees never to have traded. Many of the company registration services are located in London: if speed is of the essence, and London is accessible to you, the formalities for transferring the company can be completed while you wait; alternatively, most services will supply by return of post. In choosing between made-to-measure or ready-made you will want to consider these distinctions.

- A company formed to your instructions can be incorporated with your choice of name; the pre-formed company comes with a name devised by the registration service. Because of the numbers involved, almost certainly this name will be something boring and undistinguished; companies with commercially attractive names are available, but expect to pay a premium. Once you have acquired a company it is possible to change the existing name by employing the prescribed procedure and paying another fee to the registrar of companies.

- The company is only empowered to do that which is authorised by a document termed the memorandum of association. This document sets out what it is that the business seeks to achieve or the objects of the company. In practice, today objects clauses are so widely drafted that for most purposes this does not place much of a limitation on the company's activities. With a made-to-measure company the objects clause can be drafted to your specific requirements.

- Speed of acquisition – you can be the director of your own ready-made company today; for the company formed to order the work performed by the registration service will be in addition to the procedures performed by the companies registry.

A solicitor will register a company for you, although you may find that they in turn use a company registration service; likewise, your accountant. Do-it-yourself packs are available from booksellers and some business stationers: the saving may not be as great as it seems once you have added in the registration fee payable to the registrar on incorporation. A ready-made company can be purchased through a registration service for around £100; a company formed to your order will cost slightly more. If you don't want to buy Very Boring Name Limited, the more commercially attractive the name, the more you can expect to pay. Which brings us on to your next task: like most proud parents, when we give birth to a new business most of us enjoy the task of choosing the **name** for the newcomer.

Day five

It may be appropriate for you to trade simply under your own **name** – or it may not: ABC Burglar Alarms may be more commercially attractive than Barrie Hawkins Burglar Alarms.

If you choose to trade under a name other than your own, such as ABC Burglar Alarms, you must disclose to those who deal with your business who is behind the name. When you order the printing for your stationery your letterheads must state, in addition to the business name, the name of the proprietor or, if it is a partnership, the names of all partners. In the case of a company, as we have seen, your company will be registered with a name: just as a human being has a name, so too does a company. And just as a human being need not trade under their own name, so a company may also trade under a name more commercially attractive. Thus, in the example we used earlier, Jason has chosen to operate as a sole trader and has adopted the business name, Relyonme Mobile Mechanic. If he had chosen to operate his business through a company and bought Very Boring Name Limited the company could also elect to trade under the banner Relyonme Mobile Mechanic. Just as Jason as sole trader would be required to disclose his name on his business letter heading, so the company must likewise state its registered name.

The requirement of disclosure of the name of the proprietor, partners or company behind the business name extends to beyond business notepaper: the relevent name must also be disclosed on other documentation, including orders for goods and invoices. If you are using premises to which the public has access, you are also required to display a notice on those premises, similarly identifying the individuals or company behind the business name.

While on the subject of disclosure, note also that now you are in business you must let those who buy your goods or services know it is a trader they are dealing with and not a private individual: that this is so must be clear from your advertisements. If you take a full-page advertisement in your local newspaper pronouncing 'Sale! 300 Lounge Suites must be cleared! All stock must go!', it is clear to the reader that you are in business. By contrast, a small, classified advertisement for a single item may leave the vendor's status in doubt: it is for this reason that it is common to find the advertiser has inserted the word 'trade' in such an ad. In some trades it is not uncommon for a dealer – particularly if he operates part time – deliberately to conceal his trade status: a surprising number of 'private' sales of second-hand car bargains are anything but. This common practice often stems from a misguided desire to avoid the obligations placed upon a trader by consumer protection laws.

If you mislead your customer into the belief that they are making a purchase from a private individual, the customer will probably be able to set the transaction aside under the misrepresentation laws and you may have committed an offence under the trade description laws for which you can be prosecuted in the criminal court.

A company is subject to additional disclosure requirements: the order forms and letter heads for example need to include the number allocated to the company on registration and the address of its registered office.

As well as a business name or a company name, you may also wish to have a brand name for a particular product or range of products. A manufacturer of pet foods, XYZ Pet Foods, may be happy for each different item in the range to carry the XYZ business name. More likely, a brand name will be adopted and XYZ's customers will look for 'Smiling Dog' products. He might well use different brand names for different products: 'Smiling Dog' brand for one range and 'Prizewinning Dog' for another, the differing brand names each being appropriate for a different segment of the market.

CHOOSING A NAME

One option is for the name to relate to the product or service: 'Squeezeme' dishcloths, for example. In many eyes this is now a somewhat dated approach. It has also the disadvantage that when the name has established goodwill it cannot then be exploited to introduce other unrelated products: the 'Squeezeme' name may be of little benefit if your business expands into pottery mugs.

Many familiar names are quite short. Notice the names of some of the successful Japanese consumer electronic giants: Sony, Sanyo, Sharp. A shorter name is likely to be easier to say. A longer name which is difficult to pronounce might imply exclusivity and lend itself well to a product aimed upmarket.

Make it distinctive!

Make it memorable!

You cannot choose a name which would mislead the public into believing they are buying the products or services of a different, established business. If your product is to be socks, you cannot trade as Marks and Spencer. The lawyers term this passing off. Neither can you trade in socks as Merks and Spancer – a name so similar as to mislead customers will also find you on the receiving end of a solicitor's letter. This is not to say that an established business has a monopoly of use of a name over all trades. For example, Granada may be used by one company in relation to motor cars and by another company in relation to televisions, if the public will not be misled into believing the new product is also the product of the established producer.

Day six

Sort out your **insurance**. For most of us, insurance is not an exciting topic; few of us daydream about buying ourselves a new insurance policy. But having enjoyed the pleasurable task of dreaming up a name for the new enterprise you are creating, turn your mind now to the necessary consideration of insurance. If you plough back your profits into stock and your van with your stock is stolen off the driveway, insurance will assume a new importance. Some business people running small businesses have the attitude that if you haven't made a claim you have wasted your money. Not so: what you have bought and received is peace of mind.

You need now to look at insurance from two angles: new insurances you need to take out for the business and the effect running a business may have on your existing insurances.

NEW INSURANCES

Depending on the type of business you will be running you may need insurance for:

- product liability – what if, for example, your product injures a customer?

- stock

- equipment – what if your computer is stolen?

- occupier's liability – what if a visiting sales representative slips on a loose stair carpet?

- goods in transit

- premises

- injury to customers – while visiting a customer at home you spill a cup of hot coffee over them?

The recent huge rise in the number of claims has led to a corresponding increase in premiums: you will have to weigh up whether for a small business with limited resources the premium can be justified for the particular risk involved. Many insurers offer small-business packages: a single policy covers you for a menu of risks, from which you make a selection appropriate to your needs. Some businessses will require special insurance: if you are trading in used cars you will need a dealer policy to cover you when driving a car from stock. With some insurance you do not have the choice of whether or not to take cover: if you have employees, even if only part time, you must have insurance to cover you against claims by them for injuries caused during their employment.

EXISTING INSURANCES

'The less you tell them the better' is a guiding principle that will serve you ill in your dealings with insurers. Yet, alarmingly, it seems to have become part of the accepted attitude of the public at large towards insurance companies, along with bumping up the claim by including a dent on the car that was already there. Yet the bigger the claim the more likely the insurers will investigate the policy: so if the day comes when you really need the insurer behind you, facing a huge claim, that is when your economy with the truth is most likely to leave you unprotected... You have a duty to tell your insurers everything which a reasonable and prudent insurer would want to take into account in deciding whether to accept the risk and in fixing the premium. You also have a duty to notify the insurers if a change in such circumstances occurs while the insurance is in force.

House insurance
Notify your insurers if you are using your home for business purposes.

Car insurance
Probably your cover is for social, domestic and pleasure – notify if you now require business usage.

Doubtless you will not be surprised to receive notification of an increase in premium!

Day seven

On the Seventh Day you may rest.

CHAPTER SIX

Sources of help

Counselling you to beware the twin dangers of prevarication and delay is not to urge you to rush into your project without giving all due consideration to the implications of what you are doing. Of course you must consider the logistics and what it is you wish to derive from your undertaking.

Reading *How to Run A Part-time Business* is part of that process. But take the benefit also of the advice of friends; consider what they feel about your ideas and plans. But sift through their advice and do not be afraid to reject their opinions: you have to rely upon your own judgement.

Seek out also the advice of professionals. Here are some sources of help.

1. The Small Firms Service, a function of the Department of Trade and Industry. A source of free information, including literature on most aspects of setting up and running a small business. Address and telephone number of your nearest office is in your phone directory.

2. The network of **Local Enterprise Agencies**. Usually funded by banks, local authorities and the business community, the extent of services provided varies, but nearly all offer a range of services, with the accent on local and regional data.

3. Many local authority colleges, evening institutes and universities offer **short courses** on business start-ups. Many of these are held in the evening, offering opportunities to mix with like-minded people, to exchange information and ideas. If you are lucky your group will engender an atmosphere of mutual support.

4. **The accountant.** Whether or not it is an economic proposition for you to use the services of an accountant for a part-time business depends in part upon the scale of your business operations and in part upon what your total income from all sources will be once the income from your business is added in. If your operation will be very small, perhaps only a source of pin money, the professional fees of an accountant would be likely to swallow up an unbearable chunk of your earnings.

As regards answering to the Inland Revenue for your business activities, if your profits for a tax year are below £10,000 you are no longer required to submit a full set of accounts for the Revenue's inspection. You will need to enter on your tax return the total profits from your business for the year in question. You must be prepared to substantiate this figure from the records you have kept, your receipts and other documentation. An accountant acts as a buffer between you and the Revenue: corresponding with the Revenue on your behalf, including dealing with their queries. Some people who run a small business will, if asked, admit that they find it a source of security – even comfort! – to have an accountant on their side. They find it reassuring to have the accountant to telephone if the brown envelope contains a nasty letter.

What your accountant charges depends in part on where they are located: expect higher fees if you live in a more affluent part of the country. Based on the author's experiences of small businesses operated in the provinces, it seems possible that the annual accountancy fees in respect of a small part-time business could be less than £300, assuming relations with the Revenue remain uncomplicated.

You may need an accountant's advice on whether you are required to register for VAT. You will recall that you are under an obligation to register when your turnover reaches a specified figure. But there is also an obligation to register when you have reasonable grounds for *believing* it will do so, even though you have not yet reached that figure. It is on this latter point as it applies to your particular trading circumstances that it may be reassuring to seek professional advice. Details of VAT registration procedure are found in the booklet, *Should I Be Registered for VAT?* obtainable from your nearest Customs and Excise VAT office – address in the phone book.

Not everyone calling themselves accountants holds a professional qualification. An individual who describes him or herself as a chartered accountant or a certified accountant does hold a recognised professional qualification, and will thus have undergone training and passed the necessary examinations. For the newcomer to business the distinction between services offered by a freelance bookkeeper and those offered by an accountant can seem indistinct. The bookkeeping function is to provide a written record of the finances of the business; the role of the accountant is to interpret this and draw up from it a picture of the financial state of the business. Very often bookkeeping services describe themselves as 'accounting services', which may lead the uninitiated to believe they are dealing with a qualified accountant. In practice some bookkeeping services will be acquainted with a particular accountancy practice and will recommend the firm to their client. Other bookkeeping services may perform some at least of the functions of an accountant and draw up a set of accounts for presentation to the Revenue. For the services of such an unqualified practitioner obviously you should expect to pay less than the fees of a member of a recognised accountancy body, from whom you can expect higher standards of expertise in return for higher fees.

Most people running a part-time business will do their own recordkeeping. But a good percentage of people running small businesses find it a chore – and they put it off. Accountants whose clients include small businesses usually have at least one client whose bookkeeping system consists of dropping receipts, bills, invoices and miscellaneous papers, into a drawer. This is tipped annually into a cardboard box for delivery to the accountant, to be sorted out. An expensive system!

You should notify the Inland Revenue that you are in business once you commence trading. If you are an employee, quite probably you do not receive a tax return every year, but now you are running a business you will be required to account for your profits annually. If you find the bookkeeping side of things a chore, you may be tempted to let matters slide. If you fail to notify the Revenue you have commenced trading and your record-keeping system is the stuffed drawer, it may be two or three years before you come to sort out your accounts for the first time. Then you will have to face sorting out piles of invoices, receipts, credit notes and other papers, trying to remember what they were for – a nightmare.

From the stationers you can buy simple, all-in-one account books. Each page is divided up into columns with printed headings: somewhere for you to put down this figure and that figure. Resolve that you will make up the book at a regular fixed interval, no longer than once a month. And keep a record of the purchases and other costs you incur from *before* you start trading, as these may be allowable against tax.

Your accountant will also advise you as to your liability to pay national insurance. A self-employed person pays a flat rate contribution, plus a percentage of taxable profits if these are above a given figure. If you believe your earnings from your business will be small, bearing in mind it will be a part-time operation, you may apply for exemption from the flat rate contribution.

5. The lawyers. It is often said that the best advice to give a person needing the services of a solicitor is for that person to ask friends and acquaintances to recommend a good solicitor. In practice you may not find it so easy to find a friend or acquaintance who is ready enthusiastically to endorse their solicitor!

Amazingly – for those of us acquainted with the profession – times are changing in solicitors' offices and barristers' chambers. Piecemeal but revolutionary change has been imposed on the profession. A spirit of competition can be discerned. Solicitors are absorbing the lessons of the marketing people.

Both solicitors and accountants will advise you on the important question as to the form your business should take; we have considered this already in Chapter 5. It may well be that when you have read Chapter 11, which gives you an introduction to the law surrounding your business activities, you conclude that your business will need to use standard terms of trading in its dealings with customers, a matter to which we return in the final chapter. The devising of such terms requires the services of a legal expert. Do not be tempted simply to copy the documentation or business terms of a competitor. Most obviously, they may not be wholly applicable to your operations. Beware! Should you feel that this objection does not hold true in your case, that the terms and conditions used by another business, or its paperwork, will meet your needs, then heed this warning: the law changes, and the 'terms and conditions' of a business similar to yours may have been drawn up years ago. By 'lifting' the wording of others you may also be in breach of copyright.

Bear in mind that you will be seeking out a lawyer to advise you on business matters; seek a recommendation from a friend or acquaintance who uses a solicitor in their business. As the law becomes ever more complex, within the solicitors' firm, increasingly, individuals specialise; expect therefore to see an individual with expertise in commercial matters. A sole practitioner with a general practice – not common today – is unlikely to generate sufficient commercial work to accumulate the experience and expertise found within a specialist department of a larger practice.

Is the person you see a qualified solicitor? The work of unqualified or trainee staff is required to be supervised but, as you would expect, the standards of supervision vary widely. Does the practice strike you as businesslike? There are still examples to be found of solicitors' offices with peeling brown paint, dimly-lit passageways, frosty receptionists and rickety chairs in the waiting room. The firm with a sizeable commercial clientele may not always be the most expensive: expertise results in your solicitor spending less time in looking up matters in his law books.

6. Training and Enterprise Councils. A recent development. Funded by the government, these are local providers of business training, guidance and support. Much of what is offered to new businesses is either free or at subsidised cost.

7. 'One-Stop Shops.' A new development. A planned national network of business centres providing advice, information and support. Aim: a one-stop comprehensive source of info. Look out for news of these in the press.

CHAPTER SEVEN

Money

Perhaps you are starting your part-time business because you are looking for something to fill up your leisure hours. Or perhaps it is to see if you like business. Or perhaps it is to give an outlet to your creativity.

Or perhaps you need the money.

If income is your main objective, you are likely to be only too well aware of the irony that to get that which you need – money – takes money. Quite possibly you have hesitated up to now to start a part-time business because of the need for expenditure – even now, reading *Your Own Part-Time Business*, you may still be unsure. . .

Can you find £50? You can be in business with that level of start-up capital.

I have done it.

The arithmetic was:

Manufacturers' samples (refundable) £15
Letter headings and business cards   £20
Classified advertisements (prepaid) £15
                                     £50

Of course, you cannot start a business building oil tankers

on £50, but then that would hardly lend itself to part-time operations anyway.

Most business ideas will require rather more capital than in the above example, but fortunately there are quite a few ways of funding a little business. Before looking at these, we need to work out...

How much will you need?

Question people who have set up their own business about their experiences and ask them what tips they would pass on about aspects of the start-up or running of the business. 'Get the money in' is the advice I have received most often.

For the newcomer to business it may be difficult to perceive that a business can make profits and yet still go under. If your customers are slow in paying you, you have to find the money to pay your creditors. If your biggest and most profitable customer keeps you waiting four months before they pay your account, you cannot keep the phone company waiting four months before you pay their account: they will cut the phone off. Your own supplier refuses to process your current order until they have been paid for goods previously supplied and now you are in danger of losing a profitable order... So you incur an overdraft, on which you pay high interest rates and other hefty bank charges.

Your cash flow is all important. Cash flow refers to the money coming into and going out of the business. Money due to you must be rolling in for you to pay it out again on your bills. We look at steps you can take to minimise this operational problem in Chapter 16. But in working out the finances of your business, you may need to make allowance for money due to the business coming in more slowly than it should.

Money

You will need finance for the following.

- Start-up costs, such as the costs of forming a company.

- Acquiring assets which the business expects to use and retain for some time (termed fixed assets), such as office equipment. The capital required for fixed assets is known as fixed capital.

- The regular outgoings of the business, such as payments for petrol, telephone, stock. The capital needed for this is known as working capital.

How much working capital you will need depends on how many sales you make, and how long it takes to convert the cash laid out on stock and other outgoings back into cash again when the customer pays you. You can see how this works by taking the following totally unreal example. You purchase £30 stock on the first day of each month on 28 days' free credit. Your sole outlay for the month is £10 petrol costs, payable in cash, purchased on the same day as the stock. You sell all your stock within 21 days, your customers paying you cash on delivery. You pay your supplier at the end of the month. The working capital required for that month is £10.

But let us make some alterations to the picture. If your supplier requires you to pay for stock on delivery, the working capital required will have gone up to £40. Or, if your supplier allows 28 days' credit, but your customers do not pay you until the fifteenth day of the month following, your working capital required for the month is again £40.

In your real-life calculations you will have to add in all the other outgoings that come with real life such as phone bill, electricity and insurances.

Since you are not yet in business and making sales, in order to figure out your working capital you will need to estimate how many sales you will make in a given period. The market research you carry out (see your Action Plan at the beginning of Part B of this book) will help you come up with a figure that is not based solely on hope. Your Business Plan (also the Action Plan section) should include figures forecasting your cash flow for perhaps the first two or three years, probably broken down month by month. Once your business is operational, you (and a lender!) will be able to check the forecasts in your plan against actual receipts and outgoings to gauge whether or not you are on target. As the months go by, your forecasts can be adjusted for the future in the light of actual performance.

A further important component in all this is the size of stocks that you will hold, which will of course depend upon your sales.

Sources of finance

Many newcomers to business think immediately of the bank as the source of finance for their start-up. Experience has taught me that this is partly due to the widespread assumption that a sizeable capital sum is needed to set up a new business. With a part-time business especially, this may not be so. And when you have drawn up your calculations of how much you will need, look at them again. Think of the interest rates. You are running a business to product profits: interest on the loan can eat them away. Let us cut down the £££ you need to set up.

1. Do you really need to spend £900 on that item of office equipment? A recent arrival on the small-business scene is the telecottage. Quite possibly you have seen the birth of an example of this technological phenomenon announced in your local paper: there are now almost fifty telecottages around the UK, many of which have recently formed themselves into the Telecottage Association. You will recognise and spot a telecottage if you look for a centre bringing together a range of electronic workplace facilities which would be beyond the reach of every small-scale entrepreneur to provide for their individual business. Don't expect to come across the species if you live in a city: the phenomenon is for rural areas. If there is a telecottage in your area you will have access to information technology services such as electronic mail, desk-top publishing, spreadsheeting, copiers, fax, printers and databases. If any of these are as yet unfamiliar to you your local telecottage will be delighted to explain what is involved: telecottages provide training in the use of information technology facilities. For many small enterprises an intangible but real benefit is the contact with other individuals working alone.

Many of these centres are the result of initiatives by Training and Enterprise Councils or Local Enterprise Agencies, and financial backing has come from a variety of interested sources such as the Rural Development Commission and local authorities – so you should find the charges involved reasonable. The Telecottage Association will tell you if there is a telecottage in your area yet: address and telephone number in Appendix A.

2. You may be accustomed to buying new when it comes to buying items for your home, but could not your needs for a photocopier or computer, or whatever, be met by a reconditioned model at a fraction of the price? Especially consider buying used when it comes to equipment, machinery and fittings for your particular trade. In many trades specialist suppliers offer reconditioned machinery, such as that industrial sewing machine you are considering buying. Track down sources of equipment from business closures. Are you considering a catering business? The cost of commercial kitchen equipment will raise your eyebrows – but so too will the prices fetched for it at auction eighteen months later when that new restaurant folds. Scan your local and regional newspapers for auction announcements. Quite possibly much of what you see in the auction room is there on the orders of the administrator or carried there by the bailiff; if you do not like the feeling that you are cashing in on somebody else's misfortune, consider the positive green aspect: you will make good use of its remaining lifespan.

Having done what you can to contain your start-up costs, here are some more ways of financing your business.

- **Savings?** It may not be a permanent hole in your savings: make a loan to yourself, repayable from the profits of the business. But if this is your rainy day savings it would be prudent not to count on the business being able to return this capital. In setting up a business you are taking an entrepreneurial risk: consider *dipping into* your savings, not *emptying* the pot. If you expend all your savings on a business that doesn't work out, you will not have the income you are hoping for *and* you will have spent your capital. Possibly you have some form of assurance policy with a surrender value that you could cash in early? Bear in mind, of course, that the surrender value in the early years may not equal the sums invested and this could prove an expensive form of finance. One other possibility is to use such a policy as security for a loan.

- Could you, to use the language of the financiers, **liquidate an asset?** Most of us have some item that we could, and ought to, sell, but have never got round to doing so. Perhaps some gadget that proved to be a disappointment? Or the only extravagant impulse purchase you ever made, lying in your attic ever since, hardly used? Or something bought for a project or hobby for which enthusiasm has faded?

- An investment by relatives, or friends, or acquaintances, or colleagues at work? Such an **investment by others** need not be in the form of a loan. We considered in Chapter 6 the possibility of forming or buying a company in which relatives could buy shares without exposing themselves to liability for the debts of the business. Perhaps your parents could sell their shares in British Gas and reinvest in shares in your little business, merely exchanging one investment for another. One other tempting advantage of using a company is that the lump sum you need, which may be more than a single investor is content to risk, could be constructed from numerous sales of small blocks of shares to friends and acquaintances happy to gamble, say, a couple of hundred pounds. But be ready with a polite refusal to the individual who offers to buy a fiver's worth: every new shareholder also contributes to the administrative workload.

- Your **customers** may help finance your business. We shall be looking at when and how you should seek prepayment from customers in Chapter 14. You should certainly consider requesting a deposit if your business is one where orders require you to make an outlay on materials in order to carry out work for the customer. A part-time business in London making cakes for weddings and other special occasions requests a deposit of 50 per cent with order; the proprietor reports that in four years of trading only a 'handful' of customers have quibbled at this.

- If your business is products rather than services, your biggest recurring expenditure will probably be on stock, in which case **supplier credit** might keep you financially afloat. Many suppliers require payment X number of days after, say, invoice date or date of despatch. For others the system may be that for orders placed during a given period, payment is due X number of days after the end of that period. Depending on a supplier's credit arrangement, strategic timing for the placing of orders by the business can put some elasticity in your cash flow. For example, a business supplying and installing door entry telephones in an area with high crime rates requires customers to place a deposit of 25 per cent on signing up. The balance is payable on installation, which is usually seven to ten days after order date, this balance being collected by the proprietor when carrying out the work. Payment by the business for purchases of its phones is due to the supplier on the eighteenth of each month, payment being for orders despatched during the previous calendar month. Thus, for orders despatched by the supplier in the first few days of the month, the business enjoys almost six weeks' free credit.

Of course, it is possible that the supplier with more liberal credit arrangements may not offer prices as keen as are obtainable elsewhere. Indeed, the prices of any supplier granting credit can be expected to reflect the cost of doing so: if your goods are of the type that can be purchased from a cash and carry operation, this should provide the cheapest source. However, include in your calculations petrol costs incurred in travelling to your supplier: there is also the use of your time, and perhaps wear and tear on your nerves while you sit in traffic jams. With a part-time business especially, time will not be limitless and you may have to accept that you cannot always deal with the cheapest supplier.

The bank? If you do turn to your bank, the likelihood is that you can expect:

- them to want a written business plan. They would

prefer to see and consider the plan before the meeting with you;

- colour brochures telling you how helpful they will be and perhaps some 'freebies';

- as a rule of thumb, the loan not to exceed 50 per cent of the capital of the business;

- they will be looking not just for evidence of the technical skills necessary for your particular trade, but also business and management skills;

- if you need some of the finance for premises, such as to buy a lease, the person on the other side of the desk may have been out to visit them before your meeting, to gauge their suitabiliity and size up the locality;

- the bank may see your actual monthly or quarterly cash flow figures once you have commenced trading, so they can compare them with your projections in the business plan.

If you approach the bank for start-up finance what you are seeking is a medium-term or long-term business loan. An overdraft is intended as a temporary arrangement and presumably you will not complete paying back start-up costs in a matter of weeks or months. Do not expect the person you see in the 1990s to be the bank manager: most banks have assistant staff with a title such as 'small business adviser' or something similar.

Here are some examples, drawn from actual interviews, of questions asked by the person on the other side of the desk:

'Why did you choose this particular trade?'
'Do you think this is a good locality for this particular trade?'
'You are aware of the drawbacks in this particular trade, are you?'
'Have you got sources of supply for this?'
'How are you going to make potential customers aware of your existence?'

Will demand for your product/service be seasonal? Work out what effect this would have on the demands made by the business on your time. Ditto your cash flow.

Some of the other usual sources of start-up finance may rule out a business which is not a full-time enterprise, although it might be a different matter if operating part time is to test the water with a view to a possible later conversion to a full-time operation. With some sources a part-time operation may be too small an enterprise to attract their interest. This is likely to be true, for example, of venture capital organisations. The venture capitalist invests in risk-taking enterprise, holding shares and participating in some way in the management of the business. They look for a return which reflects the risk and subsidises the percentage of losses which they suffer in failed enterprises.

Depending on the scale of your planned business, it may be worth your while enquiring about these other sources of finance at your local enterprise agency or the nearest office of the Small Firms Service. These will have up-to-date and local information on finances such as grants and business loans from sources other than banks.

PAUSE FOR THOUGHT

The bank or other professional lender will look for security for their loan: assets against which they may have recourse in the event of failure to meet repayments. If you are a home owner, this is the obvious form for the security to take. My friend did this. He said, 'Don't worry, I'm going to make sure the business doesn't fail.' From the first nasty letter to the repossession lasted seventeen months. I saw him the day the realisation dawned upon him that he and his family really were going to lose their home. I listened while he talked for almost four hours of his worry and the humiliation he felt. I resolved that I would warn other people when they are carried along on a wave of optimism and anticipation.

If your little business fails, it is a disappointment and you will have to find another way of earning some pennies. If, to finance your business, you need to put your home on the line, and your business fails, it is a disaster.

Don't marry yourself to one business idea. Move along to an alternative idea which doesn't need so much money. Indeed, whether or not you are putting up security, consider this advice: if the noughts after the £ sign on your investment make it difficult to sleep at night, then try another idea that asks for only a small investment. You may be able to accumulate some of the profits from that to use for your Big Idea at a future date.

That's a better idea than risking opening the door to the bailiff.

April will not be the same for you

We cannot leave the subject of money without mentioning the dreaded word: tax. The spectre of the Inland Revenue has already been raised in your Action Plan, where the comfort of using an accountant was considered.

As an individual you pay tax on your income. When you operate a business, tax is payable, not on the money received by the business, but on the profits of that business. The profit is the surplus you have produced after deducting your expenditure. But for the purposes of paying tax, the Inspector of Taxes must agree that that expenditure was for the purposes of the business. In practical terms some expenditure from your bank account will be personal expenditure, such as your weekly food shopping, some will be for the business, such as the cost of this book, and some will be incurred partly for yourself and partly for business. An example of the last might be a repair bill on the car, where you use your car both for private use and for the business. In strict legal theory an expenditure is only allowable and not counted as part of your profits if it is 'wholly and exclusively' for the purposes of the business, but the Revenue, like a business, operates in the real world and recognises that part of a bill for the repair on the car should be allocated to the business, since part of the wear and tear has been due to the business. Thus, some of your expenditure will be apportioned as being partly for business purposes and partly for your personal benefit. This is especially relevant where you will be working from home and some of your electricity bill, for example, has been run up by using the spare bedroom as an office.

For the purposes of recordkeeping life is much simpler if you can operate a second bank account especially for the business, making payments for the business solely from that account. In practice, life is not so simple and you may be juggling your finances: there may be nothing in your business account the week you get a final demand for a bill for the business. But as soon as you begin incurring expenditure for the business – including pre-launch expenditure in contemplation of the business, e.g. this book

– think: RECEIPT! You will save yourself hours of time when you come to make up your accounts – or hours of your accountant's time – if you write on the receipt whether it was for a cash or cheque payment, the cheque number and the purchase, unless this is already clear on the face of the receipt.

Your accountant will tell you whether any particular item is allowable for tax purposes: if in any doubt, obtain and hang on to a receipt. Broadly speaking, the usual expenses of running a business can be set off, such as

● transport;

● maintenance of premises;

● rent;

● cleaning of premises;

● printing;

● heating;

● stationery;

● telephone;

● electricity;

● post;

● insurances;

● bank charges;

● interest on a business loan;

113

- subscription to trade journals;

- subscription to professional associations;

- wages;

- carriage costs;

- repairs to equipment;

- consultancy fees;

- solicitor's fees, e.g. for debt collecting;

- cost of business trips, such as hotel expenses;

- advertising;

- training costs.

Earlier in the chapter the distinction was made between outlay on assets which the business expects to use and retain for some time (termed fixed assets), such as a wordprocessor, and the regular outgoings of the business, such as payments for telephone and petrol. As regards the expenditure on fixed assets, for the purpose of computing your profit, this is subject to special rules relating to calculating the depreciation of these assets. These adjustments will be made by your accountant when drawing up your accounts.

If you operate your business through the medium of a registered company, the same rules apply in determining whether expenditure is deductable for the purpose of tax. But the liability will be to pay corporation tax, the arrangements for collection of which differ from those for income tax. Bear in mind also, as we have seen earlier, that if you work for the company as a director payments made to you will, like an employee of that company, be subject to the operation of the PAYE system.

Business History No. 4: *Connie C*

Field of Business: *Wholesale Distributors*

'I searched and searched for a business idea and couldn't come up with one that would suit my situation,' Connie recounts. 'I never planned to go into this field and I'm grateful it's turned out so well.'

Connie's daughter, in her late twenties, is mentally disabled and lives at home. The need to help look after her daughter restricted Connie's choice of business.

'One day I was looking through the magazines at the newsagents and I picked up one called *The Trader*. I had never seen it before and I flicked through it. It was packed with advertisements from, I should think, hundreds of suppliers, for all kinds of lines. A lot of them were wholesalers but some of them were importers and manufacturers. I had never seen such a range of goods advertised. I had been toying for some time with the idea of getting together a team of agents who wanted to earn some extra income, people who worked in a factory or somewhere with a lot of others that they could sell to. But I hadn't fixed on a particular line, and when I saw all these sources of supply I thought that I would try a number of different lines from different suppliers and just see what sold. Fortunately I had the capital put by to be able to do this.

'Originally I thought that we would have to sell at prices a lot below what people would pay in the shops but I found we didn't have to offer huge savings: a little bit of discount

115

seemed enough. We think that part of the explanation for this is that agents take the goods in to work when the staff get paid, whether this is weekly or monthly, and because they see something nice and they've just been paid, the people want to treat themselves.

'We deal in lines where the retail margins are usually quite good, such as toys and clothes. We add on our own margin, and the agent adds on a margin of 15 per cent, and we are still able to shave a small amount off the retail price you might expect to pay in the stores.

'The biggest drawback is that with most people who reply to our advertisements for agents, although they may start off quite well, after a few weeks sales drop off and it isn't worth our while to deal with them.'

In the last year or two Connie's business has found increasing competition from sales representatives who call at factories and offices, particularly on trading estates. A number of companies who sell books in this way are now well established, and the idea has spread to other lines, including pictures, wines, tapes and jewellery. The representative leaves a range of items with reception, which employees examine in their coffee break or lunch hour. The receptionist makes a note of their orders and collects the money for the representative.

This is reaching the same market as Connie's business. Her operation also shares two other characteristics with firms working in this manner: she is going *out* to customers, instead of waiting for customers to come to her, and the business does not have to bear the overheads of retail premises.

'What I could never have foreseen was that this little business has spawned another. My son and his wife now have their own business. They started part time, and last year reached the stage where my son could work full time in the business, although his wife continues to work in it part time only — there isn't yet enough income for the

116

business to support them both. He had wanted to give up his job for a long time, he hated it, but he probably would never have taken the risk.'

One of Connie's more successful lines is hosiery. 'We didn't plan to specialise in tights: our range just grew. We started with the ordinary, everyday mesh tights, and added to it items such as pop sox, and then fancy tights. Then our most successful agent surprised me by persuading a friend of his who had a small shop to stock our range of tights. We paid the agent a fee for this introduction and he saw another opportunity to earn for himself: he wanted to see if he could get other shops to take our range of tights as well. I was very sceptical.

'Within a year we had built up a round of some forty retail outlets that we supply. My son was already helping me on the agencies side by coming with me to do the buying and making most of the deliveries. He could see after a short time the wholesale side of things was more than I could cope with − I can't work full time − and eventually we split that off and he took over the running of it, although I remain a partner, having put in the capital.'

Analysing why Connie has succeeded in growing a small business that has managed to supply shops and other retail outlets, one factor that stands out is that the business supplies tights to outlets that had not previously stocked this line and do not themselves deal with trade sources supplying the line. For example, her outlets include two shoe repairers, four hairdressers and several garages. Another factor is that outlets are not required to pay for stock until it has been sold, stockists being supplied on a sale or return basis.

'Sometimes I'm still surprised that retailers we supply don't buy from the same sources as us, although I've come to realise that many small businesses don't have somebody to mind the shop while they go out and do their buying, and they wait for suppliers to approach them.

117

'I would say to anybody who was in the situation I was in
— not able to come up with a business idea that suited me
— have a go at *something*. You never know where it will
lead.'

CHAPTER EIGHT

Premises, premises

Of all the major needs of a part-time business, premises can be the easiest to provide for – or the most problematic.

Perhaps you have, on tap, awaiting useful occupation, a spare room at home, ideal for your business needs – or perhaps premises are essential for your part-time business: but who has heard of commercial premises being let out only part time?

If you cannot work from home, the need for commercial premises is not a bar to your business idea. The experiences of others operating part-time businesses affords a variety of possibilities. We shall look at these later in this chapter, but first ask yourself this question: are you positive you cannot operate from home? Could you not at least give your infant business some room at home until it is on its feet?

Your home as head office

If lack of space is the impediment to working from home, reconsider how many square feet you really need. In your full-time job you may occupy a grand office, to which you have become accustomed but, at least in the early stages of your own enterprise, could you not manage with a desk in the corner of the bedroom?

On the basis that necessity is the mother of invention, it is possible to create the space if needs be. Consider these.

- A desk and cupboard in the hallway or on the upstairs landing.

- Your garage. Possible objection: like most people's garages it is full of clutter. Possible solution: some of this could be sold off at a car boot sale and the cash put towards the business start-up costs. The remainder can be shared between the rubbish tip and the loft.

- A 10 × 8 garden shed on a concrete base, lined with insulation board. You will be surprised how acceptable this cost-effective office is – my first book was written in its entirety using such accommodation.

- A caravan.

For some of these you may need planning permission, which we shall look at shortly.

The saving in rent undoubtedly makes working from home an attractive proposition – but there may be a price to be paid in other ways. It may be difficult to insulate yourself from the business when you are not working on it: you may find yourself remarking on how amazing it is that customers choose to telephone you the moment you sit down to a meal. Actually, it is not so surprising: they ring you at home at meal times because that is a good time to catch you in. Depending on the nature of your business, there is also the possibility of callers at your home when you are in the bath. If you register for VAT a Customs and

Excise officer will carry out a periodic inspection of your books: you may not like an official coming into your castle. Note also that if you choose to claim a proportion of the outgoings on your house as an expense of the business you are running from it, in order to reduce your tax bill, this could give rise to complications with capital gains tax. A rise in the value of your house is normally exempt from this tax because it is your home, but if you attempt to make a tax saving also on your business profits by claiming business use, it is open to the inspector to make a proportion of any gain in value subject to the capital tax. Since the problem only arises if you choose to claim a proportion of your house expenses against the profits of your business, this need not be a bar to electing to operate from home, but this tax aspect is a matter you should consider with your accountant.

Some of the disruption to your home life can be minimised by the use of an accommodation address. For a few pounds per month your letter heading can boast a prestigious address in London's West End or the City. Mail is forwarded at agreed intervals or can be collected if the accommodation address is located near enough; the need to forward mail on to you extends its time in the post. Many accommodation addresses also offer a telephone message service: consider whether this could be an adequate means of dealing with calls, taking into account the type of calls you are likely to receive. If you use an accommodation address, but give your own telephone number on business stationery, customers may wonder why you have an Eastbourne telephone number for an address in Oxford Street, London. One other possibility is to use a post office box number, but a percentage of your customers may not like dealing with you if they do not have an address at which they can call, even if they never need to do so.

Working from home can have the disadvantage that it reduces your contact with other human beings. Many individuals ploughing their own furrow encounter a sense of isolation: they come to miss the camaraderie of the office or factory. If yours is a business where home is simply a base from which you operate, you may get plenty of human contact: calling on customers at their premises, for example. But that in turn requires you to draw on your self-discipline: with your own business there will be no boss waiting to bawl you out if you do not turn out on time on a cold, misty morning.

Possibly you don't have a workplace to which you go at present, if you are retired for example or are at home looking after the children, so you don't have a feeling of camaraderie to lose. But working at home, as opposed to living at home, will make demands on your self-discipline even if you haven't got to go out on the road on a frosty morning. It's easy to put off getting down to work as there's always something that needs doing about the house: a letter to write, a bulb to change, a lawn to mow. And friends who are at home during the day will ring you now that you are also at home during the day. You will be tempted to allow the mechanic to come and mend the washing machine while you are there, who may be only too ready to chat.

If you do encounter that sense of isolation, try and make contact with others running their own small business. Join the National Federation of Self-Employed and attend meetings of their local group. Ditto the local chamber of commerce. Look out for small business courses run by your local college. Draw on your local knowledge to come up with other ways in which you could rub shoulders with other small entrepreneurs.

PLANNING PERMISSION

We observed in your Action Plan how some newcomers to business labour under the delusion that having planning permission for premises somehow confers a licence to operate a particular business. Planning permission actually relates only to the use to which premises are put.

If you change the use of premises, you may require permission from the local authority to do so. You already have planning permission for your house (presumably!) to use it as a domestic dwelling – if you are now also to use these premises for business purposes, will you need planning permission for change of use? The answer given here cannot be a definite yes or no: whether or not you need planning permission for such a change must depend upon your particular circumstances.

Probably millions of people use their home to some extent for the purposes of a business and do not need planning permission to do so. Permission is needed for a 'material' change of use. At one end of the scale permission will certainly be required if the premises are no longer used primarily for domestic purposes. At the other end of the scale the self-employed insurance agent almost certainly does not need planning permission to use a study for a few hours each week to make up books. Is the use of the premises for business purposes substantial? Factors the planning officer will look at include whether or not there has been a marked rise in callers at the house: are you displaying your range of garden sheds to a succession of prospective customers? The planning officer will also be influenced by the volume of traffic caused by your business activities, such as deliveries. In one case, a choose-at-home carpet service arranged with suppliers for the delivery of customers' carpets to be made to the proprietor's address, to avoid problems with customers who were not at home to take delivery. Enormous, noisy delivery lorries regularly blocked entry and exit to the cul-de-sac location, enraging adjoining occupiers...

And this brings us to another popular misconception: that a grant of planning permission for a business authorises those carrying on the business to make whatever disturbance is necessary to operate from the premises.

UPSETTING THE NEIGHBOURS

Planning permission authorises lawful use; it does not sanction an unlawful nuisance.

You may be liable for unlawful nuisance where your activities cause a substantial interference with your neighbours' use and enjoyment of their property. If business activities carried on at home generate noise, smell, smoke, fumes or vibrations, you could find yourself on the receiving end of a solicitor's letter – all of these have been held by the courts to constitute unlawful nuisance. Of course, all of us experience some of these to some degree from time to time – the smoke for example when a neighbour burns their garden rubbish – and adjoining occupiers will only have a legal grievance if what you are doing amounts to more than a reasonable person could be expected to tolerate. Much could depend on locality: as one judge put it, what would be a nuisance in Belgrave Square would not necessarily be a nuisance in Bermondsey!

In practice, many proprietors of small businesses operated from home give no thought to planning permission until they learn that a neighbour has complained of their activities to the local planning department. Better to write or telephone the planning department before launching your business, setting out for them the use you have in mind and seeking advice as to whether planning permission is needed. I have heard a planning officer observe unofficially that planning departments have been encouraged by HM government to be 'supportive' of small businesses who are struggling to take root from the proprietor's home address. A sympathetic, generous interpretation of the planning laws could give way to a stricter interpretation once your new business has a foothold. The planning authority for an area is the district council.

There exists also the possibility of what the lawyers term

a 'covenant' in the deeds of your property, which could be used against you by an antagonistic neighbour. In particular, it is not uncommon with modern housing estates to find the deeds of the property include a clause inserted by the builder prohibiting use of the property for business purposes. An identical clause is usually inserted in the deeds of each house on the estate; so if this applies to you, your neighbour will know from their own deeds that you are subject to such a restriction. A participant on a business course I ran had recently set up from home a small business breeding puppies: her business activities came to an abrupt halt when she received a letter from a solicitor acting on behalf of her neighbour asking if she was aware that this amounted to breach of covenant.

If you live in rented accommodation, do you need the landlord's permission to operate a business? It is possible a clause in your tenancy agreement either prohibits any business use or makes it subject to the landlord's permission. Better check your copy of the agreement. . .

Commercial premises

If your business idea is one which leaves you no choice other than to operate from business premises, the $64,000,000 question is, of course: how can a part-time business support a full-time overhead? Landlords do not rent out shops, offices, warehouses, for only part of the week. The part-time entrepreneur is faced with a disproportionate financial burden – and an underutilised asset. Or are you? Only you can answer this, because only you know what is to be your own personal definition of part time. The active individual who has taken early retirement at fifty-five after thirty years of five-day-week working may relish the luxury of dropping down to a four-day week. Paying the rent for a fifth unused working day may seem a small price to pay for the luxury of a three-day weekend.

This disproportionate overhead will eat into your profits, but it may be that you are able to undertake a part-time business activity because you need only to generate a modest financial return. We have all seen the small shop, located away from the High Street, open on only the busiest days of the week, probably including Friday, Saturday and market day.

Others who have come up against the obstacle of finding *affordable* commercial premises have found their own way around it.

WORK OUT A DEAL

Seek out premises that are **not for rent**. By all means pursue the usual channels such as the commercial property column of your local paper, and agents, but to turn up a property at below the usual market rent you will probably need to wrap up a little deal that is out of the ordinary. Somebody out there has spare capacity, but they have never offered it to rent because of some complication or other. Perhaps there is a complication over accesss, or security, or the need for permission to sub-let. Perhaps this problem is not such a problem for someone who only needs to use the premises for part of the time. Or perhaps to secure accommodation you are prepared to be a more accommodating tenant.

Do not be put off by the attitude of commercial agents. You will probably not dare to tell them the tiny rent you can realistically pay. Yes, most of them would smile and shake their head. But, be assured it can be done: it is possible to unearth modest business premises that will be offered to you at a very modest rent. Consider how the economic recession of the late 1980s and early 1990s has caused many firms to cut back on their activities, very often shedding staff in the process. An example is the legal profession, where staff numbers on solicitors' firms contracted along with the volume of conveyancing carried out as the residential property market slumped. Your local high street accommodates dozens of small businesses and professional practices in office accommodation located above shops: is it not possible that one of these firms now has an empty room or two on the top floor? Talk to people. Trail the possibility before your insurance broker, the local employment agency, your accountant. If your friends and acquaintances do not include such business contacts, talk it over with them in any case: you may not know your babysitter's father, but he or she knows him! You may discover that their father runs a small business: might he have a room or two which is underutilised? Don't ask your babysitter to ask – it is too easy to brush off such an approach coming through a third party. This needs personal contact. *You* need to put your case; in the process giving your quarry the chance to hear and see what a reasonable tenant you would make.

It is demoralising to confine yourself to a nightly search of the classified columns of the evening paper in the hope that your bargain-priced accommodation will appear tonight. Take the initiative and insert your own advertisement. By all means use the business columns of local papers, since a proportion of business people are always interested to see what others are advertising, but do not dismiss that most inexpensive of media: your newsagent's noticeboard. If this is not a medium you have ever used, you may be in for a pleasant surprise. A heavily used board is not confined to advertisements for missing cats and second-hand pushchairs: the noticeboard for a busy shop may have fifty cards. Don't write out just one card! Put a card on every noticeboard you can find in the area. Make your card stand out: use a coloured felt-tip pen; draw something to catch the eye – perhaps a smiley face.

Such a card might also be a way later of getting custom for your business.

SHARING THE PREMISES

We are all familiar with the idea of flat sharing or house sharing – if we are prepared to **share** our home, why not transplant the idea to commercial premises?

The proprietor of a recently established part-time consultancy business was discussing the problems of accommodation with her accountant. With two children under five she was reluctant to work more than two days a week, but was finding in her field of work that seeing clients at her home detracted from the image she wished to cultivate. She could not believe how often one of the children was sick on the carpet shortly before a client arrived. Her accountant, having set up his sole practice the previous year, understood the problems of operating solo: to win himself a client base, he was offering to visit busy clients, which left an empty office to greet personal callers. The accountant's office was a huge room in a Victorian building. The same thought came into both heads at once: there was plenty of space at the opposite end of the room for another desk and a filing cabinet. Two enterprising individuals, two problems – one office, one solution.

You may be able to take the concept further. Useful office equipment, such as photocopiers and faxes, become much more affordable if the rental charge is halved. And, going one stage further still: this might make a secretary feasible. A part-time secretary, perhaps mornings only, might be sufficient help to meet the typing needs, while covering the phone.

Just as sharing premises may be the answer for your new business, it may also be the solution for other embryonic businesses. As an alternative to trying to squeeze into someone else's business premises, consider uniting with another new entrepreneur to hunt for premises you could take on together. This could be a further benefit to be derived from joining a business start-up course. An evening course on which I taught at the local college usually enrolled some thirty to forty 'students'. Perhaps the ambitions and problems of one of these individuals would dovetail with your own. This links in with our next possibility for solving your accommodation problems...

FINDING A PARTNER

The need for putting a roof over the head of your little business could be another good reason for **taking a partner** along with you on your new venture.

Let us suppose you turn up some premises offered at a very reasonable rent, a figure that would justify less than full-time occupation, say four working days per week. You have two days each week to devote to business, although the business you have in mind could operate at a scale that justified four days' work. Your friend, Jane, has more time on her hands now that her child has recently started school and...

If you haven't a friend like Jane, you might meet someone like her on one of those business start-up courses. If your nearest college tells you they run such a course only once a year starting in September and it's too late to join, don't end your searches there. Such courses may be offered by further education colleges, university continuing education departments, evening institutes, training and enterprise councils, and local enterprise agencies: one might be starting next week! Don't just try local sources: ring round throughout the county – and the next county: with a short course you wouldn't have to undertake the journey many times and could put up with travelling a long distance – bearing in mind the benefit you are going to be deriving from owning and operating your own part-time business.

READY - PACKAGED ACCOMMODATION

What is often termed **service accommodation** is a form of shared accommodation that comes ready packaged. This comprises a suite of offices with a central reception and switchboard, whose services are shared by the individual tenants. Very often, office equipment such as photocopiers and fax machines are provided centrally for communal use. Your telephone is answered and your callers welcomed for a fraction of the usual cost of providing your own staff. Many such suites welcome brand-new businesses, offering very small units of accommodation at a rent which reflects the lack of floor space. But whatever the size of the unit, each tenant must bear through their rent their share of the overhead costs, including staff.

MOVING PREMISES

Would premises with wheels suit your needs? Go to where the customers are with your **mobile premises**. Caterers follow the crowds to outdoor shows and events, serving customers from the self-contained trailer hooked to the back of the car: if they can transport a kitchen, can you not transport the accommodation you need to serve your customers?

This is not just a means of reaching the general public: in many trades wholesalers bring a mobile showroom to clients, especially to small businesses faced with the problem of who will look after the shop while the proprietor is away doing the buying. Jewellery, toys, clothes, greeting cards, fancy goods, giftware, video tapes, small electrical items and records are all supplied to retailers by wholesalers who prefer the running costs of a van to the rent and overheads of bricks and mortar.

Commercial premises: what is involved?

If your decision is to go for commercial premises rather than working from home you will need to consider a few points.

First, if you are entering into a lease, what is to be the extent of your obligations? A lease grants the right to occupy premises for a specified number of years: if you are being granted a new lease, you will agree the term (the duration of the lease) with the landlord. However, it may be that you are taking the transfer of an existing lease, in which case you are taking the tenancy for the years remaining under the original term. This does not necessarily mean that you will have to vacate the premises when the lease expires, since in certain circumstances the law gives tenants of business premises security of tenure: the landlord may be required to grant a new lease on the expiry of the existing lease.

Where you are taking over a lease, the obligations will be those agreed between the landlord and the original tenant; if you are being granted a new lease, the terms are open to negotiation. In practice the landlord's solicitor may offer a draft lease which pushes a list of responsibilities on to the tenant, including maintenance and repairs: depending on the state of the building, over a period of years, the tenant might be faced with a succession of bills for work on a property the tenant does not own.

Naturally, if you are taking a lease you will consult a solicitor. Do not assume that the terms offered are the norm and that by querying them you are showing your ignorance of business terms. If this is your first venture into business, make sure your lawyer is aware of this and does not overestimate your understanding of the extent of the obligations. Be absolutely certain that your proposed use of

131

the premises is permitted by the terms of the lease and make sure there are no restrictions that would prevent you carrying on your business in the manner you propose; for example, remaining open during the evening.

You may find you are asked to pay what is called a premium: this is a capital sum payable on taking the lease. This is less likely in times of economic recession when tenants are more scarce. If you take on a lease for an agreed number of years and wish to leave before the expiry of that term, unless you can secure the landlord's agreement to release you from your obligations, which is extremely unlikely, you will need to find a successor to take over the tenancy, assuming the lease permits assignment.

Some local authorities offer what is often referred to as 'nursery' units for start-up businesses. The object of the authority is to encourage the development of new businesses in its area and a common feature of such accommodation is the 'break clause'. This is a term which permits the tenant to withdraw before the expiry of the agreed term.

Secondly, taking premises currently used for business purposes does not free you of planning considerations. Planning permission is not granted for general business use, but for a particular type of business use. If, for example, existing permission is for the premises to be used for the storage of goods, you would need permission to use the premises as a shop. Not all changes of use, however, require permission and the planning officer will give preliminary advice as to whether permission would be needed and the likelihood of its success. If planning permission is needed you can expect four to twelve weeks' average wait for the outcome, depending upon your area.

Thirdly, considerations as to location may restrict your choice of premises. If your business will depend on passing trade – potential customers passing the premises – location is crucial. If your trade is of a specialised nature, such as spare parts for vintage cars, your customers will be more willing to seek you out.

The location and address can have a role in the image the business wishes to create in the minds of customers: an address in Mayfair may convey expectations of high prices and deter potential buyers; but such an upmarket address would suit very well a prestigious product of superior quality. The address will influence the buying decision whether or not the business is one where your customers call at the premises: with a mail order operation, for example, customers may be reluctant to post orders and sums of money to 'Basement Flat'.

CHAPTER NINE

Your sources of supply

A young man decided to start his own business. Interested in electronics, together with a partner he began assembling tape recorders, working in a small shed. The man still works in his business. The business is Sony. He was once asked what was the recipe for the astonishing success of his company, its explosive growth into a household name multinational whose operations and reputation span the world. This is the company which devised the biggest selling consumer electronics product of all time, the Sony Walkman. The man, Akio Morita, now chairman of his company, replied, 'Have good products'.

He added the instruction to make the products well. Sony manufacture their products, and possibly your business will be making that which it sells, although on a somewhat smaller scale. More likely, with a part-time business, you will be buying in your product. You will be relying on others for your product.

Where will you find these good products?

Even if your business is a service business, the likelihood is that customers will receive from you more than your labour: the part-time washing machine repair service will supply replacement components.

Will they deal with you?

We touched upon this subject in Chapter 2, where we considered the possibility that large companies may wonder whether your orders will be big enough to justify dealing with you.

Whether or not suppliers will supply is a question which, from my experience of business start-ups, troubles many of those who are new to business. It does so to an unnecessary degree.

Although many newcomers to business worry that suppliers will turn them away, my experience is that a percentage risk creating the problem for themselves. I have been surprised that some individuals setting up a business will send out initial letters of enquiry to prospective suppliers that are handwritten on a sheet of lined notepaper from a cheap writing pad. Some suppliers, especially small businesses, will respond, but what an impression this letter will create: that the writer, not committed even to spending a few pounds on a business letter heading, does not have serious intentions.

Setting up a small business, our objective is to generate income, perhaps much needed, and I understand the hesitation to lay out money. Those who have not been in business before may regard their venture as akin to gambling. A state of nervousness may better describe the condition in which some newcomers view the prospect of any expenditure on fulfilling their dream. But presentable headed notepaper and a supply of business cards sufficient to get you going can be yours for less than £20 from small, mail order printers. Drawback: you will have to wait for the postman to receive your inexpensive business stationery.

A dozen or more suppliers advertise regularly in the columns of the *Exchange and Mart* (*E & M*), published weekly on Thursdays. If this is a publication which hitherto you have passed over when scanning the newsagents' racks for something to read, you will discover that for the small business on a very modest budget it can mean the difference between to have and not to have. You ring round local suppliers for that piece of office equipment that would make life easier: the prices you hear were not intended for your budget. In *E & M* you find that a firm in London supplies reconditioned models at 40 per cent of the price. (You might also turn up a wholesale supplier of the product you sell, but as with other journals do not confine yourself to the sections devoted to trade supplies. You could write to advertisers selling retail to the public, enquiring whether they supply the trade.)

The question concerning you upon which a prospective supplier will need reassurance is: can this customer pay?

You may find their method of doing business is to open an account, under which goods are supplied, settlement of the account being made in accordance with the terms of trading. In this case, you will be expected to complete a form requesting the grant of credit facilities and supplying the names and addresses of referees. Commonly the suppliers will stipulate that these referees should be trade references, other suppliers with whom you hold or have held credit accounts. Very likely they will ask also for the name and address of your bankers. Obviously, if you are new to business, you will not be able to supply trade references. Some suppliers offer the alternative of making payment with order for a stipulated number of transactions, to establish ability to pay, after which an account will be opened. If you have no trade references and this alternative is not offered, it is open to you to write to the supplier and explain that as a new business you will be happy to prepay a given number of orders. Such a letter might also be the answer where you are setting up your part-time business because the income is so much needed that you hesitate to give your bank as a reference. If you do not wish to parade that you are new to business, you could write to the prospective supplier informing them that instead of credit facilities you prefer to have the benefit of a discount for prepayment and would they please let you have details of this.

One or two suppliers to whom you write your initial letter of enquiry may never reply. This probably has more to do with the inefficiency of business than the circumstance that they have never heard of you. The process of establishing relationships with suppliers can be disconcerting. Some will reply to your enquiry stating that their representative, Miss X, has been asked to contact you, but she never does. Some will reply that their representative, Mr Y, will contact you when he is next in your area, and he telephones to say that this was last week and he will call in two months' time. With others, you return home one day to find a business card left by a representative who has called without informing you that he or she was coming. If you are expecting suppliers to be delighted to receive an enquiry from a prospective customer and to cultivate your business, many will disappoint you. But unless you are dealing with a product with few sources, there will be some suppliers who strike you as efficient, with good products and providing the information that you need.

Tracking down suppliers

Work your way through the following sources.

1. **Directories of suppliers**, which can be found in the reference section of public libraries. These list suppliers by trade. Be forewarned that the copy held may not always be the latest edition and that some firms listed may have moved or gone out of business.

2. For just about any trade you can name there will be a **trade journal**. Your public library can help here also: almost certainly the reference section will hold a directory of journals published in the UK. Some will be available on subscription only, in which case telephone or write to the publisher asking for a sample copy and subscription details. In the case of journals available from your newsagent, ask them to order a copy of the current issue for you.

    In addition to the hundreds of titles aimed at a specific trade, a few titles carry advertisements from suppliers across a broad spectrum of products. *The Trader*, for example, is a monthly carrying hundreds of advertisements from suppliers of fashions, toys, jewellery, hardware, fancy goods and giftware, usually at the cheaper end of the market, and aimed at market traders and discount shops.

    In some trades you will find a number of titles, each aimed at a different sector of the trade, so do not assume that the first title you come across is the only journal published for that trade.

3. The Department of Trade and Industry via its **Small Firms Service** will supply, on request, lists of manufacturers, importers and wholesalers for a given product. The address and telephone number of the Service's head office is given in Appendix A or, as mentioned earlier, the telephone number of the nearest regional office can be found in your local telephone directory.

4. Joining your local **chamber of commerce** might help overcome the sense of isolation that can be felt by the proprietor of a small business, ploughing a lonely furrow. Supplier contacts might be made at meetings and the chamber will pass on to members details of

overseas suppliers who have approached the chamber looking for business contacts themselves.

5. Trade journals will carry news of forthcoming **trade fairs and exhibitions** where you can meet row upon row of suppliers. The journal will give details of how to obtain entry; a complimentary ticket may be included with an issue, especially if the event is sponsored by the publishers, or exhibitors may supply complimentary tickets to customers. Expect to be asked to complete a registration card at these trade-only events, giving the name and address of your business and your position with the firm. You may be presented with a name badge in return, telling the world the name of your new business. Take with you a supply of your business cards to give out to exhibitors you wish to be in contact with after the show.

6. Suppliers listed in **Yellow Pages** may not be restricted to your local area: it may carry names of firms based in other areas but who do business in your patch.

Dealing with suppliers

If tracking down suppliers can be disconcerting, so may your dealings prove to be. Small suppliers in particular, oblivious to their obligations under the law of sale or contract law, may cause you to raise your eyebrows. (Matters of which *you* will have a sharp awareness after reading Chapters 11 and 13.) If your work experience has not caused you to have dealings with trade suppliers, to pass on a warning now of what you may anticipate will help to lessen your annoyance, surprise and disappointment when any or all of the following occur.

First, you will be dealing in quantity. If you buy an item as a consumer there is a possibility that it will be defective; if you buy a stock of 100 of these as a trader, then the chances of a problem are accordingly 100 times greater.

If you buy, say, an assortment of seventy-five digital watches, you may find that two or three do not function. You *may* find that seven or eight do not function. Probably the supplier's standard conditions of trading will have something to say about the terms under which they will accept returns: do not assume that this is binding upon you; after reading Chapters 11 and 13 you will be better able to judge whether the restriction placed upon you by the terms is valid. In some trades it may be customary to expect a given percentage of items in a bulk purchase to be unsaleable. Much will depend upon the price. If you buy 500 assorted watches at 30p each – quite possible if you buy one of the journals aimed at market traders – the importer may think you are naïve if you attempt to return 2 of them as faulty. In these circumstances you must build into your prices a margin to cover the costs of stock you discard.

Secondly, you may have to be wary of passing on to your customers descriptions of goods made by your suppliers. Suppliers in some trades display a breathtaking disregard for the accuracy of their product descriptions.

A mis-description can occur easily where the specification of the goods changes. The first batch of digital watches your supplier imported last year were accurately described as gold plated; the consignment which has recently arrived are finished in gilt, a change made by the Far East manufacturers to reduce costs.

And, finally: excitement! The carrier delivers your very first stock order. Item number seven on your list was three dozen widgets in autumn gold. They are missing. But you have a box of orange sproggets that you did not order – or did you? You did make a copy of the order for yourself, didn't you?

They've made a mistake. You ring them to complain and ask them to send the widgets. You make your long-distance call and the person you want to speak to is on the other line. No, it wasn't a mistake, they were out of stock of widgets and sent you sproggets instead.

If they do this once they'll do it again. Quite possibly they have orange sproggets in stock because they do not sell very well in that colour. You have the choice of going to the bother of packing up orange sproggets and sending them back, or keeping them and hoping that they will sell. You decide to keep them and manage to sell one or two over a period of time, by which time your suppliers have sent you substitute items on a number of occasions.

You can instruct your suppliers on the phone not to send substitute items in future, but this sort of firm will forget what you have said or the person you tell will leave the company. You will have to mark each order at the top 'No substitutes please', and underline. The puzzle why you have got sproggets instead of widgets may be cleared up by the invoice: look for the words 'substitutes' or 'out of stock', if you can read the writing and assuming the orders clerk has remembered to make a note on the invoice or delivery note. And assuming that they supply a detailed invoice or other breakdown of your order: today some suppliers, to save labour and thus costs, send a receipt, invoice or whatever with just a general description such as 'goods supplied'.

Lack of continuity of supply can be a recurrent source of exasperation. There is rather more to success in business than a product which sells profitably. You are well pleased to find that customers love your widgets in this new shade of green. But your suppliers are out of stock. They are out of stock *because* the line has sold so well. And you will despair when your supplier withdraws a line from their catalogue and does not tell you. You have worked hard to make a sale to your customer: the customer places a firm order with you and you order the item from Idiot Suppliers Ltd. Now you make the discovery that the customer's order is no longer available. The customer has placed the order with you, not with your supplier: it is you who has to break the disappointing news to your customer. In their eyes it is your business that has let them down. You may well be in breach of contract. I hope you will not shrug your shoulders and live with this situation. This is not 'quality service', either on your part or on the part of your suppliers.

What can you do in an endeavour to maximise continuity of supply? Even if you have found what you consider to be the best source of supply, you should consider keeping a second supplier in tow. Perhaps the alternative supplier has the same lines at higher prices. But if you have an account with Alternative Supplier Ltd and place an order with them occasionally to keep the account alive, you may be able to avoid disappointing your customer when Idiot Suppliers Ltd let you down. Not buying all your widgets from one supplier's basket may be a part of the price you pay to be reliable.

CHAPTER TEN

Another pair of hands

If I could read your mind as you read this book I would know the scale of business operation you are planning. If your plan is for the tiniest of operations, a few hours each week, for some useful additional income, you may be tempted to skip this chapter: 'I don't need anybody else'. Are you sure? We considered earlier the problem of who will answer the phone when the proprietor of this part-time business is pursuing a full-time job, or taking the children to school or whatever. Ditto who will answer the door to the delivery person. And the proprietor of even the smallest operation can be ill, and the colds and flu season begins conveniently in the run up to Christmas, which is very likely to be your most profitable trading period. Then again, while your wish may be not to involve others, are you sure you can perform all the functions yourself? Sales? Buying? Admin? After-sales service? Record keeping?

My experience is that the first thought of the individual launching a small business is that free labour is to hand in the shape of the family, probably their spouse. Beyond this, the automatic thought is to take on employees. If employing staff is also your natural expectation, pause here.

Especially think again if you have been put off a business

idea because it would involve others and you equate this with employees. Let us find for your part-time business some alternatives to the obligations, duties and responsibilities of being an employer. And let us start with perhaps the least obvious.

Your competitor

In Chapter 2, where we looked at the type of business that lends itself to part-time operations, we considered whether this included a business whose customers expected round-the-clock service. Taking as an example a business offering a maintenance service for heating systems, I posed the question: what happens when your customer rings on a freezing winter's day to say the system has broken down, just after you have left home to set out for your full-time job? Here is a possible solution: an acquaintenace in the trade who agrees to cover for you. But how much cover will that person have to provide? Our example – a business offering twenty-four-hour service and a proprietor who also has a full-time job – is an extreme one. For a business offering a lower level of service, or where the boss does not have the ties of a full-time job, a friend in the trade, pleased to fit in some extra work now and then, might suffice.

Possible drawbacks to the solution: using the contact with your customers, will your 'friend' attempt to steal them? As they are not your friend's own customers, will they get the same quality of service or will they have to wait until your friend has finished watching the football? The key to overcoming these unwanted complications must be reciprocity. Provide a reciprocal service for your friend's small business. Such an arrangement is a necessity in some types of trade, whether operated part time or full time, where customer demand can be subjected to a sudden surge: for example a one-person taxi or car-hire service whose Regular Customer No. 1 needs a car which is already booked for that time to Regular Customer No. 2. In rural areas the small taxi/car-hire service is often an example of a business where the proprietor has other commitments, probably because there is insufficient demand to sustain a full-time service. But life being what it is, it is a safe bet that after the phone has been silent for several hours, it will then ring twice with two 'jobs' at the same time. The chances of disappointing the customer are much reduced thanks to a friendly arrangement with the taxi service in the next village.

Keep it in the family

A ready-made source of free labour. Your other half can answer the phone. And can do the books for you.

Or so I have been told by a lot of folk new to business.

It does not work for everybody. It did not work for me. I found that, like the proverbial lunch, using the most important person in my life as labour did not come free. Using free labour, 'just until I can afford to pay', you will have to learn to bite your tongue. If you can sense the 'I'm doing you a favour' attitude then you are not doing your business a favour: won't this come across in the tone of voice they use to customers on the phone?

Remunerating a conscripted member of the family is not necessarily a cure-all for the problems. The employee who is not giving satisfaction is subject to the company's disciplinary procedure: a warning, an interview, a ticking off. If you haul your loved one over the coals for being late for work, you might find you eat your evening meal together in silence. Or you might not get an evening meal at all: you might be too busy bathing and putting the kids to bed on your own.

And when he or she goes off to deal with that customer you suspect is going to be awkward, as soon as he or she has gone you may wish you had done it yourself.

But it may work for you, if you are using your big, strapping, ugly brother.

Or perhaps, instead of master and servant, the awkwardness could be removed from the relationship if the labour of this member of the family was the labour of a business partner?

A partner

The idea of a prospective partner has raised its head in other chapters, and we have considered various pros and cons of taking one on. My experience is that money looms large in the mind of many partners: your partner is taking half your earnings.

And you are taking half of *your partner's* earnings.

But if you have need of labour, a person that you hired would have to be paid. Ah, you will say, to pay a hired hand the going rate won't hurt my pocket as much as a partner taking a slice of the profits.

But remember you will also have your partner's intangible input, the sharing of responsibility with you. And the partner's labour may be in the form of some valuable service: the sales and marketing function for example. But then again, you might be able to buy this in from time to time as you need it, from a freelance.

146

If you have someone in mind as a business partner, reflect on what you consider to be their main skills and abilities. Then compare these with your Personal Profile and consider the extent to which they complement your own.

The professionals

Almost all businesses buy in labour at some time or other: the professional services of the accountant or solicitor. In Chapter 3, trying to come up with an idea for a business for you, we considered setting up as a consultant. We noted the generous fees you may be able to command if you have the nerve to ask for them; now, as the prospective customer, you are faced with paying those fees. But the Department of Trade and Industry and many Local Enterprise Agencies have schemes for small business under which they meet part of the costs of consultancy services. It still may not be cheap, but the value of advice from someone who really knows their field could be incalculable. In a society in which education seems to take longer and longer, it may also be a revelation how much useful, practical, valuable, relevant knowledge can be handed on in a few days or hours by an individual who knows their stuff, has done it, and can communicate it. They are out there. But, of course, so too are those who will disappoint you; in my experience, almost always the individual not long in the consultancy game. They do not get the repeat work or recommendations and they do not last.

You can buy in aid across the range of management

functions, in technical aspects and, increasingly, with your 'personal development': from personal image to public relations, from advertising to exporting, from new products to new sales techniques, from time management to team management, from handling change to handling clients.

But a business does not just buy in the services of the Professional with a capital P, but also the services of the window cleaner: an individual who carries out work for the business, who is not an employee, but an 'independent contractor'.

Independent contractors

An employee is a person who performs work for another, their employer, in return for payment. A person who performs work for another for payment but who is not an employee, such as a window cleaner, is an *independent contractor*. If you have been an employee you have enjoyed the benefit of an increasing battery of rights conferred on employees by Parliament in modern times: the right not to be unfairly dismissed, the right to redundancy compensation, the right to maternity leave etc. But when the state creates a right for one party, an obligation is created for another party. Much employment protection legislation does not apply to part-time workers, those working fewer than sixteen hours per week; but the moment you become an employer – even in the smallest way – some obligations and responsibilities are placed upon your shoulders that you cannot decline. Did you know, for example, that an employer is liable in civil law for the wrongs committed by an employee in the course of employment? So, if you take on a part-time employee, just for a few hours, and due to *the employee's* negligence a customer is injured, *you* are liable. (Hopefully you did not skip the section on insurances in the Action Plan, because you thought the topic too boring.) But if the window cleaner drops a bucket on the head of one of your customers it is pretty safe to assume you will not be liable. These independent contractors serve you in both your personal life and your business life: at the workplace the people who decorate your office, who call to repair the photocopier, and deliver parcels for you, are examples of fellow human beings performing work for you, who are very probably not your employees. These are examples of services which all businesses may require, but the concept of using an independent contractor can be extended beyond these: could not a particular need of your business be met in this way?

Let us say you set up a small business supplying fitted carpets. Your mode of operation is a choose-at-home service. You enjoy the sales function and have a good conversion rate (the conversion rate is the percentage of enquiries you convert to orders). You have basic DIY skills, feel capable of carrying out the fitting work yourself – but you have only a limited number of hours per week to devote to this business. You advertise under 'Sits Vac' and take on a part-time employee to fit carpets. Now you have to operate PAYE. And will you always have enough work for the fitter, or might they be collecting a full pay packet while 'knocking off early'? But turn to a different section of the classified advertisements and you will probably find an advertisement placed by someone offering to refit carpets. You give the advertiser a ring, and that person agrees to fit carpets for you at a trade rate. You will give the fitter an agreed number of days' notice for each job. In the week between Christmas and New Year you make no sales, you have no takings, the fitter doesn't have a 'job' to undertake for you – as he or she is not your employee you haven't got to pay the fitter to sit at home. But when the sales come in, you pay the fitter from the proceeds of the sale – the reason your commitment has arisen is *because* you have made a sale.

There must be a flip side. Well, you don't have the same degree of control over a self-employed contractor: if you, as proprietor of this carpet business, telephone in the run up to Christmas you may find that the fitter cannot fit in your work. There may not be the same degree of commitment: unlike an employee your contractor does not have the incentive of promotion prospects. But then, the employee of a part-time business is hardly likely to be planning to make it a lifetime's career.

It would be very unpleasant if one day the authorities decided that a contractor was in their view your employee. What if, horror of horrors, you receive a letter from the Inland Revenue seeking arrears of PAYE they claim you should have deducted over the last few years? Plus the employer's national insurance contributions? I have often been asked, 'How can I be sure that the person whom I pay to do work for me won't be classified by the powers-that-be as my employee?' The answer is that you cannot always be 100 per cent certain. While in most instances it is perfectly clear one way or the other, in other cases the dividing line is blurred, very often because someone who is in reality an employee is 'dressed up' as a freelance contractor, the employee trying to escape PAYE deductions from what he or she is paid. In one case where the court had to decide whether a particular worker was an employee or a contractor, the judge, having gone through a number of tests used by the law to decide, said he might just as well spin a coin to resolve the matter!

The modern test for determining whether a person performing work for another is an employee or not is the 'indicia' test: does the person concerned have the badges of self-employment? Or, put another way, what indicators are there that the person is in business on their own account? For example, does the person carrying out work for you keep a set of books of account? This is not something a regular employee would need to do. Another useful indicator is whether the person provides their own tools and equipment.

Small business support services

In the Action Plan we looked at bookkeeping services; another routine need for most small businesses is typing. In *Yellow Pages* you will find one or more secretarial services. This could also provide a solution to the demands of the telephone.

An agent

As with consultants, we have earlier looked at agents with a view to coming up with an idea for your business. You will recall that an agent is a person who has the power to act on behalf of another, called a principal. Now we are considering whether it is the principal's role that you should fulfil. A common type of agent is the sales agent, the agent making sales of goods or services on behalf of the principal. The agent is able to enter into agreements for sale because he or she has the power to legally bind the principal.

We are all familiar with the army of agents, working in their spare time, representing the big mail order catalogues, such as Littlewoods and Grattan. The catalogue your agent works from need not comprise 1,000 pages: most of us will have seen, at some time or another, being passed around a small catalogue for, say, cosmetics or greetings cards. But the costs of colour printing are such that for most small businesses any form of glossy colour catalogue would be prohibitively expensive. Equipping a team of agents with samples could be a viable alternative, depending on the size of your product range and the value of the items. Some of the costs of equipping agents could come from a returnable deposit paid by the agent on recruitment. Realistically, however, individuals looking for spare-time income may be deterred from becoming an agent if they have to lay out money before they have earned anything. Possible solution: a retention from their earnings. Keep back, say, 10 per cent from each payment you make to them until they have built up a sufficient retention to recover the deposit. Possible drawbacks: the impecunious individual who flogs the samples and spends the proceeds before you have accumulated the deposit. But in business you have to accept some degree of economic risk.

Sales agents are commonly remunerated, of course, on a commission-only basis: no sales, no earnings. This is nice for you, because sales representatives who are employees, although usually remunerated partly by commission, will have some sort of a basic wage. But then again, if you do not have to pay the agent it is because you have not had the benefit of sales made by the agent.

Using an agent, you have far fewer obligations than if you employ someone.

Your employee

If your requirement is for a specific number of hours and regular times, taking on a part-time employee may be the only way you can achieve this.

How do you stretch the budget of a very small business so as to fund the hours for which you need another pair of hands? Try the sixth form of your local school. As a customer, you may not have much opinion of the sixteen-year-old school leaver in the corner shop that serves you and can't add up, but the bright A-level student who has stayed on at school and needs some income could be a different proposition.

Experience has taught me that teenage employees can get bored very quickly and their rate of work slows down as they do so; their mates also have a habit of turning up for a chat. But the individual who is interested in what you are doing, and whom you are able to keep interested, can be an economical source of help. But don't exploit them and do treat them as human beings. Make up their low wage rate by taking the trouble to pass on some skills.

Our society also expects to reward less generously those at the other end of the age range. Once we have officially retired our earnings capacity as an employee drops dramatically. Historically, no doubt this was due to the enfeeblement of the average sixty-five year old – who bears no relationship to today's fit pensioner looking for an interest to occupy the time on their hands. Experiments by some supermarket and DIY chains, recruiting part-time staff from this age group, are reported to have been spectacularly successful. Employers appreciate the interest these employees show in their work, and their reliability: customers appreciate their civility.

The observation has been made earlier that much employment protection legislation does not apply to those who work less than sixteen hours each week: note that the burden is also reduced for the employer who has a very small number of staff. But even if you as an employer come within these two exceptions, a rump of obligations remains. Useful booklets are obtainable from the Small Firms Service and the Health and Safety Executive; look up the nearest office of the latter in your phone book.

Whether or not the people who work with you are your

employees, you have a responsibility for their health and safety: for your legal sake, familiarise yourself with your duties; for their sake, comply with them.

Business History No. 5: *Anne Y*

Field of Business: *Security*

The telephone ringing at 6am in the morning gradually pulled Anne Y out of her sleep. She turned over, trying to ignore the insistent ringing, cursing herself for not having switched on the telephone answerer the night before. The ringing persisted: on and on. Suddenly she threw back the clothes and stomped down to the telephone, snatching the receiver off the hook. She shouted, 'What?' down the receiver.

It was a customer.

The previous week Anne's business had sold and installed a burglar alarm system which had given the householder problems ever since.

'The woman was ringing', Anne recalls, 'to say that her husband had got up in the night to go to the loo and had set the burglar alarm off, which was not supposed to happen. She said it had given him such a fright that he wanted to go to the loo again, but was too scared in case he set the alarm off yet again. Because he couldn't sleep, she couldn't sleep either: and she was ringing me because she didn't see why *I* should be able to sleep. At the time I thought she must be mad, but looking back on it now I think she had a point — the burglar alarm had been a nightmare for her.'

The telephone call proved to be a turning point in the history of Anne's business. While holding down a full-time job in telephone sales, she had set up the burglar alarm company in the light of a huge increase in burglary in her

154

locality in the preceding two or three years.

'Obviously there had always been burglaries of bigger houses and commercial premises, but burglary of ordinary homes on this scale was something new. I realised that this major change in society must be creating a need for some sort of security for the average semi-detached house.'

A book on business start-up advised Anne to look up lists of suppliers in a directory likely to be found in a main library.

'We wrote to quite a few suppliers, but some of them did not reply and with the others the product wasn't suitable for the customers I had in mind. And then I spotted an ad in a magazine, for a firm supplying simple alarm systems direct to the public by mail order. I wrote and asked for details and whether they supplied trade. The sales leaflet was so interesting that I bought a sample system. It was exactly what I was looking for. They allowed me a good discount for quantity and the minimum order was only three. I was in business! These suppliers were not listed in the directory of suppliers I had looked up.

'I didn't know whether to form a company. My solicitor advised me that if I did so my liability for the debts of the company would be limited. But unlike a person trading on their own or with a partner, the accounts of a limited company – I know now – have to be audited. This means that they have to be checked by a qualified accountant. When I received my accountant's bill at the end of the year, I thought he must have made an error. It was so high.

'I also found that I wasn't the only person who knew about limited liability. Of course! The first thing for which I needed credit was for supplies of the alarm systems. The manufacturers were happy to open a twenty-eight-day credit account – subject to the directors personally guaranteeing to make payment of the debt in the event that it became overdue. Originally I operated from home but later took a sub-lease on a small office and workshop. The landlord was prepared to grant the lease to the company, provided the directors undertook personal liability to pay the rent in the event of default by the company. So much for limited liability!

'I tried to get my first customers through advertising in the local paper. I received a call in the very first week. It was an incredible feeling answering the phone to my first enquirer. He asked me lots of questions; some of them I couldn't see why he wanted to know. He said he was from the local district council and I had a sudden vision of supplying burglar alarms to all those council properties. He arranged to call and see me the next day.

He was not a potential purchaser. He was from the Planning Department. He said he could tell from the telephone number that I was located in a residential area. The council had recently had a number of complaints about a burglar alarm company operating from home and causing annoyance to the neighbours. Clearly we weren't at the stage where we were causing a nuisance, and he went away again.

'We reached the point quite rapidly where we needed more space than I could give over to the business at home. But I was still working in my own full-time job and it seemed silly to pay the rents I was asked for commercial premises when for most of the time they would only be used for storage. I have had some amazing success in the past with advertisements on newsagents' noticeboards — and they didn't let me down this time. I put up an ad that said, "Can you help a struggling business?" I was offered the basement offices of a Georgian building at a nominal rent in return for my looking after the garden.

'I did come up with one unexpected snag. I spent quite a lot of money on a board bearing the company's name and telling the world our line of business. A few days later I received a letter from our landlord's agent informing us that, under the terms of our sub-lease, the board required the permission of our landlord, and this was refused. Eventually they did agree to a very small, inconspicuous nameplate which couldn't be seen from the pavement and was of absolutely no use for advertising purposes.

'I hadn't read the lease. The next time I took a lease I read every clause, and went through a list of things that I didn't understand with my solicitor.'

Eventually, all Anne's customers came to her via advertising leaflets. 'We raised our leads from leaflet drops. We were regularly getting between three and seven replies for every 1,000 leaflets we put out. To somebody new to business this didn't seem like many replies, but I now know that these were phenomenal reply rates. I understand it is common for reply rates for 1,000 door-to-door leaflets to be in the range of one or two per 1,000 leaflets delivered. In highly competitive trades such as replacement windows it may be only one reply for every 2,000/3,000 leaflets put out.

One of the things we were doing right was that I would scan the local paper each week for reports of burglaries and we would rush round to that locality and put out leaflets printed in red ink warning that burglary was increasing alarmingly! The householder would receive this while the news of the nearby break-in was fresh in their memory.'

In retrospect, Anne now considers that, 'I did a lot of things right but also got some things badly wrong. I loved the challenge of selling, going out and getting the orders, and coming back home with signed contracts and deposit cheques. All the rest of it — what happened after that — I was not interested in. I was terrible at administration, especially bookkeeping and VAT. Looking back I feel it would have been better if I had simply been quite good at a number of activities. I would say to anybody else in the

157

same position that it is better for you to work with a partner who can counterbalance your weaknesses and vice versa.'

Anne considers a further mistake was that, in her own words, she was not 'close to the product'. In a part-time business such as hers, or any small-scale enterprise, the proprietor can't help but be anything other than closely involved in the day-to-day running of the business. The proprietor is unlikely to employ some other person to manage the business for them, so you must be interested in the product or service you are offering.

'I had not the slightest interest in burglar alarms and absolutely zilch technical or electronic skills — even now I don't like putting on a three-pin plug.

'This was a nightmare when things went wrong. If the burglar alarm kept triggering, the customer wanted immediate attention, but because I couldn't do anything to them myself I had to rely on other people. I used a sub-contract electrician to install the alarms for me and for servicing faults, but if I couldn't contact him there was nothing I could do myself for the customer.

'I sold the business to him. We moved from the area afterwards and recently went back to visit friends: it seemed every street had a bell box bearing the name of my company.

'But I had learned that I loved running my own business. And having tasted it, I couldn't go on taking orders from somebody else. I gave in my notice and, using the money that I'd earned from my part-time business, I set up a full-time business in a different field.'

CHAPTER ELEVEN

Know some law: contracts

The solicitor was rounding off the advice he had been giving to his client seated on the other side of the desk.

'. . . and that is the position, I'm afraid,' he concluded.

Glumly, the client gazed at his adviser. He had a thoughtful expression on his face. Eventually he broke the silence.

'If only I'd known that. . .,' he said, his voice trailing off. He stood up and shuffled out.

The lawyer shut the door behind him. Then he stood for a few moments gazing into space, his turn now to pause for thought.

'And if I had a pound for every time a client said that to me, I'd be able to buy that new yacht. . .,' he told himself.

How useful is a knowledge of law in business!

Not so much because huge numbers of con artists are waiting out there to rob you – although in business you will encounter a few customers and suppliers who *are* rogues – but rather for this reason: probably *most* people, whether customers or suppliers, have no knowledge of law. If this includes the proprietor of your business, then you and the party you are dealing with wander through your transaction in blissful ignorance of the legal position, without knowledge of the respective rights and obligations of the parties. If you do not know what are your legal rights, then others may not give you what is your due – not because they are dishonest, but because, like you, they do not know what are your rights in the matter.

Law – and in particular the law which affects business – is not, contrary to the commonly held view, a dry and musty subject. We cannot, in one chapter, turn you into a mini-lawyer, but you can gain a greater awareness of the extent to which the law impinges on business activity and whet your appetite for a subject you should pursue further. The saying, 'A little knowledge is a dangerous thing', applies to law – but only if you are hopeful of picking up sufficient law to avoid consulting your solicitor when you encounter a legal problem. You will need to read more than a few law books to substitute for six years of study and training. What you could realistically achieve – and these should be your objectives – include:

● the ability to recognise the point at which your business becomes legally bound in any particular transaction;

● sufficient awareness to help you avoid mistakes that could lead to costly litigation;

● the ability to ensure that your business is acting within the law and in its best legal interests;

● a basic knowledge of the obligations of your business and your suppliers;

● a heightened awareness for detecting when it would be prudent to consult your solicitor.

Formerly I taught a short evening course designed as an introduction to business law for the small business. At the end of one course I was approached by a member of the

160

class, the managing director of a high-tech company with a turnover of some £2,000,000 per year. He told me how, for a number of years, his main supplier of components had, in his words, 'messed about'. He recounted how it was most unusual for a consignment from his supplier not to be unsatisfactory in some way, how frustrating it was that the supplier failed to pay attention to the customer's requirements. 'For years we've put up with it,' this businessman told me, 'and then a few weeks ago I told them what I'd discovered about the Sale of Goods Act and what they should be doing. I just laid out for them what their obligations were under the law. I must have sounded as if I knew what I was talking about, as since then we've only had one small problem with a delivery. And I'd put up with it for years thinking that they could just do what they had been doing. . . .'

You too may find that if you know some law, those with whom you deal in business accord you a little more respect.

The areas of law most likely to impinge upon the day-to-day activities of the part-time business are the law of contract (which we look at below) and consumer law (examined in Chapter 15).

Ask a person in business, 'What is a contract?' and the chances are the reply will be along these lines: it's a document, in writing, usually with long words, signed by the people concerned. . .

All this is correct – but only for a tiny minority of contracts.

There can be few subjects relevant to the world of business over which there is more misunderstanding than the law of contract. Yet this subject looms large in everyday business life: it is contract law which governs most of our transactions. It lays down the legal position – and thus what you should do – when buying or selling something, when having work done for you or if you are doing work for others. Here are some popular misconceptions:

- a contract to sell goods is enforceable only if the customer has paid a deposit;

- in general an agreement will be upheld by the courts only if it is in writing;

- the judge would consider it unjust and refuse to enforce an agreement to sell something at a fraction of its value.

What is a contract?

During the course of our everyday lives, both personal and business, we all agree things with other people: all of us make numerous agreements over the course of a week. We agree to meet a friend for a drink at lunchtime, we agree to put the children to bed while our other half does some work on their part-time business, we agree next-day delivery of an urgent package with a parcel delivery service, we agree with the office equipment company that their engineer will call on Thursday afternoon to repair the printer. Clearly, not all these agreements are legally binding; some you would not want to be so: presumably you do not intend to sue your spouse if you discover, after putting the children to bed, they have watched *Coronation Street* instead of working on their business. You had an agreement, but you did not have a contract, for that is what a contract is: a *legally binding agreement* – an agreement which you can enforce in a court of law.

The popular misconception of a contract taking the form only of a transaction recorded in a wordy document leads on to a further common misunderstanding. Yes, it is a contract when you sign an agreement for the purchase of a

162

van for the business on hire-purchase terms and it was a contract you signed when you bought your house. But every time you buy a Mars bar you make a contract and when you go out for a meal, get on a bus, have your hair cut, buy a paper, have the windows cleaned, get some petrol, do the shopping. Quite possibly your response is that while these little everyday transactions in legal theory amount to contracts, they are not important, unlike the contract to buy a house or a van. But what happens if that everyday transaction goes wrong? A solicitor will tell you that most clients assume that because they have suffered harm they must be able to sue somebody. This is another wrong assumption. There is no legal principle that requires another to pay you compensation merely because they have caused you harm. We all suffer harm at some time or other without being able to sue the party who caused the harm.

Let us suppose your part-time business is the selling of free-range eggs on a stall in the market place on Thursday, Friday and Saturday each week. The local theatre is pulled down and the site bought by a supermarket which, when opened, takes away many of your customers. Your business becomes unprofitable. You have no choice but to close it down. You have suffered grievously at the hands of the giant supermarket chain but you cannot sue them for your loss: you have suffered in consequence of business competition which is permitted in our free enterprise society. It would be different if you could show that a *legal wrong* had been done to you. One of the ways in which you can do this is to show that the other party made a contract with you which they have broken. It may be that what the other party has done also amounts to some other legal wrong, but one of the two or three biggest and strongest weapons for your use is the action for breach of contract. Hence the importance of knowing whether you can attach to a transaction, even a small, everyday transaction, the label 'contract'.

163

Essential ingredients of a contract

A contract may be made in any of the following ways:

- by word of mouth;

- in writing;

- partly in writing and partly by word of mouth;

- inferred from the conduct of the parties;

- by deed (a formal document, signed and witnessed).

As a general rule, an agreement need not be made in writing to be enforceable. This is subject to a number of exceptions, including where a business sells goods on credit to a consumer, but in the overwhelming majority of cases it is not necessary for the party seeking to enforce an agreement to show that it was made in writing.

If you are contending in court that an agreement you have made is a contract, what must you show? You need to satisfy the court that three essential ingredients were present. These we can label *agreement, intention* and *consideration.*

AGREEMENT

If you are going to law to claim the existence of a legally binding agreement, the obvious thing you must prove is agreement: that the parties agreed. If you think about this, where you are trying to persuade a court that someone else agreed with you, what you are trying to show is that their mind was identical with yours. Take as an example a part-time business dealing in second-hand cars. The dealer shows the car to a potential customer and says, 'This is the

Escort – if you want it the price is £2,000, I'll deliver on Friday, cash on delivery.' If the customer says, 'Yes', then an agreement exists. The minds of the seller and the buyer are identical on the matter: they are both referring to the Escort car, each knows what the price is, they both know when delivery will be and who will make it, they both know when payment is to be made. What is in the mind of one of them is also in the mind of the other – they are in agreement.

But what if the customer later denies an agreement was made? How can the dealer prove agreement? How can the dealer show that what was in one person's mind was also in the mind of another? Clever as the judge is, even if he or she were to open the customer's skull and peer inside, the judge could not read the mind of the customer.

As the lawyers cannot conclusively prove that the parties agreed and cannot show that their minds were identical, they have to settle for less. The lawyer representing the client who seeks to show the existence of an agreement has to demonstrate not that the parties agreed, but that it *looks* as if they agreed. The test of agreement is: if a reasonable bystander heard what was said, saw what was written, witnessed the behaviour of the parties and knew of the background circumstances, would that person conclude that an agreement had been made?

In practice the court usually breaks this down into two stages. First, the court looks to see if one party made an *offer*. If satisfied of the existence of an offer, the court then looks to see if the other party made an *acceptance* of that offer. An offer is a *statement of terms* by which the party making it is willing to stand.

Since the test of agreement is whether it *appears* the parties made an agreement, it is possible for a person to be held to an agreement which they did not intend to make: it looks to the court as if an agreement was made and, accordingly, the court pronounces the existence of such an agreement. How important it is then to be able to judge whether what you are saying, writing and doing amounts to that which could be interpreted as an offer or as an acceptance of an offer.

Offers
Having said that an offer is a statement of terms by which the party making it is willing to be bound, we can see that an offer is made in the car dealer's example. In the statement as to the price of the car, the date of delivery, by whom delivery was to be made and arrangements for payment, the dealer was making a statement of terms by which a reasonable person would expect him to stand.

To understand what might amount to an offer, it is useful to look at examples of statements that do not amount to a statement of terms. You have just overheard the following exchange:

> *'I've just started my own business. Do you know anyone who might be interested in helping me out on Saturdays in return for a bit of spare-time cash?' says Jason.*
>
> *Tracy replies, 'I am. Trouble is, I'm going to start a family next year.'*

Here no offer has been made by either party, but we can isolate:

- *a statement of fact* – 'I've just started my own business';

- *a request for information* – 'Do you know anyone who might be interested in helping me out on Saturdays in return for a bit of spare-time cash?';

- *a statement of intention* – 'I'm going to start a family next year'.

166

An offer, a statement of terms, is something more than any of these.

In business it is essential to recognise when something being said or written can be viewed as an offer: if it does amount to an offer in the eyes of the law, then an acceptance communicated by the other party, a 'Yes', brings the contract into being – and the parties are legally bound from the point that the contract came into being.

It will help to make clearer what an offer is if we look at what the courts have said does *not* constitute an offer.

Placing goods on display: the courts have held that merely displaying goods that are for sale does not amount to making an offer to sell them.

Returning to our example of the part-time car trader, if he places the Escort on the driveway of his house with a 'For Sale' notice on the windscreen, this would be an *invitation to treat.* By displaying the goods he is inviting passers-by to enquire about the car, to enter into negotiations.

In the case of a shop, the legal breakdown is that if the customer, attracted by a window display, enters the shop and says, 'I'll have one of those', it is the customer who makes the offer.

Since in this example it is the customer who is making the offer, the shop is free to accept or reject it. To a customer, the legal position may seem to be unreal, but if the business you set up involves running a shop you will discover that the law accords with good commercial sense. Normally you will be only too pleased to take the customer's money, but on occasion you may have good reason for not selling an item to a particular individual. For example, you may have reserved it for somebody else or it may be the only one you have in stock and it is needed for display purposes.

Advertisements: newspaper and magazine advertisements are generally also viewed as an invitation to treat, and not something amounting to an offer.

Let us suppose this time that you have set up a mail order operation. You have made a bulk purchase of 1,000 men's workshirts, made in China, an importer's end of range clearance. You book a small display advertisement in a Sunday newspaper.

Almost certainly such an advertisement does not amount in law to an offer. When your customer writes a letter to you saying, 'Please send me . . .' and enclosing a cheque, they are making the offer. Again, the supplier is free to accept or reject the offer and, again, it is good common sense. You cannot know how many orders you will receive. Imagine the situation if the legal position was otherwise, if the advertisement amounted to an offer which was accepted by the customer placing an order. If you then received more than 1,000 orders, each order placed that you could not meet would leave you in breach of contract. It is commercial common sense that the supplier should be able to reject orders and the supplier can do this because it is the customer who is making the offer. If the supplier is in the fortunate position of receiving more orders than they are able to supply, they will inform the customer that they are now out of stock and return the cheque. In so doing the supplier is rejecting an offer.

It is possible for an advertiser to devise an advertisement that does amount to an offer, but there are few cases where the court has found this to be so. It seems this will only occur where the advertisement requires those responding to it to go off and do something for the advertiser: for example, '£10 reward for any person finding and returning my lost kitten'. It would be absurd if the advertiser could say to the finder who arrived on the doorstep with the kitten, 'No thank you', and refuse to take the kitten back!

Price lists and circulars: a catalogue, circular or price list is likely to amount to an invitation to treat and not an offer.

It is the customer who makes the offer, for example, by completing an order form and posting it off or telephoning your office and leaving an order on your telephone answerer. Again, it enables you as supplier to accept or reject the offer if need be.

Acceptance
If the court is satisfied that one party made an offer, it then looks to see if the other party made an acceptance of that offer.

It is not sufficient for you to decide to accept an offer that has been made to you: that you are accepting must be made known to the other party. The general rule is that a contract comes into being, and the parties are bound, at the point at which an acceptance is made known to the party who made the offer.

You can only validly accept an offer if it is made to you. The person who makes the offer can choose to make it to the world at large, or restrict it to a group, or make the offer to just one party. If an offer is made to some other person, your purported acceptance is in reality an offer, which, like any other offer, the party receiving it is free to accept or reject.

To make a valid acceptance, the offer must still be in existence when you endeavour to accept it. A party who makes an offer is free generally to withdraw it at any time before acceptance. However, you should not find yourself accepting an offer to then be told that it was withdrawn, since to withdraw an offer validly, notification of withdrawal must be given to the person to whom the offer was made.

An offer does not endure for ever and a day, however. If an offer is not withdrawn, it will eventually die of old age. Let us suppose that your supplier makes you a special offer of some surplus stock at a hefty discount off the normal trade price. It may be that they choose to put an express time limit on the offer, eg seven days, and if they choose to do so there can be no valid acceptance after that time. In most cases, however, no such time limit is imposed, which introduces an element of uncertainty, since in the absence of such a time limit the offer lapses after a reasonable time. What amounts to a reasonable time is a question of fact in all the circumstances. If the stock offered is produce which deteriorates rapidly, should you take too long to decide and telephone in two weeks' time, the offer will have lapsed.

Contracts made by post
Many contracts made in writing are not embodied in a formally worded document headed 'Contract' or 'Agreement': a contract may be found, for example, in an exchange of letters.

We saw earlier that a contract comes into being and the parties are bound at the stage when an acceptance is made known to the party who makes the offer. Where you are dealing by post, a gloss on this rule provides a pitfall for the uninitiated. If an acceptance is made by letter, that acceptance will be deemed by the law to be communicated – and the contract come into being and the parties thus bound – from the time that the letter is put into the post. Thus, if you make an offer and the other party accepts by post, the law does not wait for you to open the letter or even for it to be delivered to you, before it deems the acceptance to be communicated. Unless you have been made aware of the acceptance by some other means, while it is in the post you will be bound by an agreement, not knowing that it has come into existence. This rule – that a letter of acceptance is deemed to be communicated when it is put into the post – is known to lawyers as 'the post rule'. For this rule to apply it is not necessary for the party receiving the acceptance to have made the offer by post; the rule applies provided it is reasonable for the other party to use the post.

What happens if a letter of acceptance is posted but lost in the post and never received by you? Will you be bound by a contract of the existence of which you were unaware?

Yes.

This affords an example of the kind of matter for which you may wish to make provision in a set of trading terms you have drawn up, upon which basis you do business. We consider whether your business should adopt its own standard terms, and the related question of using its own documentation, in Chapter 16. The post rule is an example of a rule governing the formation of contracts which can, in fact, be ousted by the parties: it does not have to apply to your dealings. Thus your terms and conditions could, if necessary in the light of your business operations, include a clause to the effect that where your business makes an offer, the agreement will not come into being until you actually receive notification of acceptance.

It will be observed that the rule that a letter of acceptance is deemed to be communicated when it is put into the post is an exception to the general rule that an acceptance must be made known to the party who made the offer. The exception to the general rule does not apply to communications made by telex: it has been held that notification of acceptance sent in this manner is not binding until it is printed up on the telex equipment of the party who made the offer. While a telex machine is unlikely to appear on the shopping list of equipment for a new part-time business, that more recent example of technology, the fax machine, may well be an early purchase. It seems quite likely that, in the case of communications made via a fax, the courts will take a view similar to that taken with regard to telex and hold that there is no binding contract until notice of the acceptance is printed by the fax machine of the party who made the offer.

INTENTION

For a court to accept that your agreement is not just an agreement, but a contract, it must find the presence of a second essential element: an intention by the parties that the agreement would be legally binding.

It is this ingredient which is missing from some of the examples of agreements listed earlier in this chapter. Thus, the agreement to meet a friend for a drink at lunchtime is not a contract, as the parties never intended it to be an agreement which they could enforce in a court of law.

With transactions made in the course of a business, however, intention to create legal relations is an issue with which the courts hardly ever have to deal. This is because with business transactions the court presumes there is such an intention. In theory, it is open to a party to a transaction made in the course of a business to argue that it was not intended to be legally binding, but it is for the party making such an assertion to prove it and it is an uphill struggle on a very steep hill! Understandably so, since one would assume that people in business anticipated their transactions to have legal consequences.

CONSIDERATION

This is an example of an everyday word to which lawyers attach their own particular meaning. And for you, now, when dealing with contracts, the word consideration does not mean being kind or thoughtful.

From the viewpoint of a party to a contract, consideration may be thought of as the 'price' paid, but do not assume from this that consideration takes only the form of money. Consideration may also take the form of goods or services, or some other benefit conferred by one party on the other. A simple example illustrates the concept. Earlier in this chapter we looked at the example of a newspaper advertisement announcing a reward of £10 payable to any person who finds and returns the advertiser's lost kitten. That the advertiser is giving consideration is obvious, but consideration is given also by the finder. From the finder's

172

viewpoint, the consideration given is the act of finding and returning the kitten: an example of consideration taking the form of services.

In the case of an agreement for the sale of an item for immediate delivery, payment to be upon delivery, consideration is given by the supplier as well as the buyer: the consideration given by the dealer is the item sold.

In practice, in business transactions the question as to whether or not consideration is present rarely comes before the courts: in the overwhelming majority of cases the presence of this essential ingredient is immediately apparent. One reason for this is that the law will recognise something quite insignificant as constituting consideration, something of tiny value. An item such as a box of matches or a copy of yesterday's newspaper could amount to consideration. As a general rule, the court will not become embroiled in an investigation as to whether the consideration given is adequate for that which was to be received in return. So in our example of the sale of the Escort car, if the price payable was £5, and the car a Rolls-Royce, the inadequacy of the consideration given by the buyer would not of itself be a ground upon which to challenge the validity of the contract. The law recognises that special provision needs to be made to protect the interests of certain categories of people, such as minors, but otherwise takes the view that it is for the parties to make their own deal.

Even today it behoves contracting parties to bear in mind the law's Latin maxim *caveat emptor* – buyer beware.

Business History No. 6: *Dennis T*

Field of Business: *Home Furnishings*

At some time in the past, while living in a different area, Dennis T's wife, Joan, had purchased a set of loose covers for a suite of furniture. The covers had begun to show their age, but the company they had dealt with had been a national company which had ceased trading. The market for loose covers had declined over a period of years, due largely to a tendency in a more affluent society to replace a suite of furniture earlier rather than give it a new lease of life, as our parents would have done. But a strong market remained among the older generation and among that sector purchasing durable, high-quality furniture.

Neither Dennis nor his wife could recall a shop that stocked furniture covers, nor could they find a supplier among the advertisements in the local paper. *Yellow Pages* listed a supplier in the next county, some forty miles away. Most suppliers of such home furnishings offer a choose-at-home service, but when Dennis rang the supplier he was reluctant to make a call involving a long trip without a guarantee that Dennis would place an order. As Dennis says, 'How could we know whether or not we would be able to place a definite order without having seen the samples?'

For someone who had been mulling over the idea of starting his own little business, here was a gap in the market. Although neither Dennis nor Joan had experience of running their own business, before taking early retirement Dennis had worked as a salesman for many years.

'The chap that we had bought our own covers from came along with a book of fabric samples, but I realised it would look as if we had a much bigger range if we broke open the book and laid out each of the fabrics separately for the customer to see. We spread them all over the floor and it makes a colourful display.'

Furniture covers fall into two main types: stretch covers, which come ready-made to fit standard styles of furniture, and loose covers, usually in heavier fabrics, made to measure for the customer's particular suite.

Know some law: contracts

'For somebody setting up in business for the first time, the obvious way to get in enquiries from customers is to advertise, and that is what we did. We worded an advertisement for the classified columns of the local paper under "Articles for Sale". It worked from week one. We made two sales in our first week and after that it regularly produced two to three orders every week. Probably two of these would be for suites, with one or two smaller orders for individual chairs. After four weeks' advertising, when we came to renew the ad we made a slight change to the wording. That week we had no replies! We telephoned the newspaper and asked them to change the wording back and the following week we had in the usual two or three enquiries. It was amazing that such a small change to the ad could make such a difference.

Once we had been getting in regular work for about six months I had another attempt at making a small alteration to the wording. Again, the reply rate fell right off; there was another hasty telephone call to the classified advertising department! We never toyed with it again after that and I see now why some of the small advertisements that appear week-in and week-out in the local paper never change.

'We have found that some customers say to us they have seen our advertisement over a period of time and it has been in their mind to give us a ring. The advertisement appearing regularly week after week seems to provide an element of security to those customers who need it. They almost feel that they are familiar with us before they telephone us. This may be of particular importance because they are inviting us into their home, and in this day and age older people especially are increasingly cautious about who they open their front door to.

'The market that we are in is middle class, plus what I would call respectable working class. Taken with the type of product that we are selling, I found that the

175

overwhelming majority of our customers were not looking for something cheap: I found the expression "reasonable prices" went down well with our customers and the expression "very reasonable" went down best of all. This was the expression we used in our little classified advertisement that runs every week in the local paper and which has done so well for us.'

From the earliest days, Dennis made the pleasant discovery that a proportion of enquiries came from people who had seen his covers at the home of a friend or relative.

'This type of enquiry is far and away the best. The prospect has seen for herself the quality of the covers and how lovely they are, and knows that we can be trusted to do a good job. It is just a question of calling to take the order. We do have a marvellous product. The firm who make up the covers do a terrific job of it. They are always a beautiful fit.

'We also give good service or, rather, what customers regard as good service — as far as I am concerned we are just doing what we have promised. We estimate to within an hour or so the time at which we will call to see the customer; on the odd occasion we are going to be late we ring the customer and let them know. We have found that customers are incredibly grateful we have done this, which surprised me. Then we came to realise, as customers ourselves dealing with other tradespeople, how often they let you down.

'I thought I would see if I could do something to encourage the recommended business. I devised a letter that I leave with customers when we finish fitting their covers. In the letter I say that as a small business we try to keep our prices reasonable but that we find advertising expensive. There is a type of customer — a big percentage of people I'm pleased to say — who like to deal with a small business, especially a local one. I found that if we talked to this sort of customer, and they felt they had got to know us, they would be pleased to try and help us.

'In our "recommend a friend" scheme I did not feel it was appropriate to offer our customers money, but rather, as I expressed it in the letter, "we would like to give them a small gift, as a token of our appreciation". So if the customer will be "kind enough to pass on our name to a friend or relative" we are pleased to present them with a pair of cushion covers to match the furniture covers we have supplied. Trade cost of this to us is only £2 or £3. Today some 40 per cent of our business comes to us in this way.

'A bonus that I had not expected is that after we have sent the free cushion covers to the customer, most of them will write back and thank us. Writing this letter presents them with an opportunity to also thank us for the quality of the service they have received and to tell us how pleased they are with their purchase. We've collected these letters together and tell a prospect that we have this collection of testimonials that they can inspect if they would like to.'

Although Dennis and his wife are free during normal working hours to devote themselves to the business, a good proportion of their calls have to be made in the evenings and on Saturdays when customers are at home to see them. 'A business like this, a choose-at-home service, would be ideal for someone who could only work evenings or weekends,' Dennis says.

'You do not need to have a lot of capital to start up a small business. I use my car for the business and work from home; we had to pay our suppliers for our range of samples, but that was about it. And we were making money from week one. The business does not make a fortune. The hours I work over the course of a week add up to about two and a half working days and, on average, even with my reduced pension, we live well. I wish that I had taken early retirement years ago.'

CHAPTER TWELVE

Getting orders: the fundamental techniques of selling

'I'm not a salesperson.'

Rubbish.

I have heard this scores of times from hesitant individuals on How to Start your Own Business courses. We are ALL salespeople. You sell yourself when you ask a member of the opposite sex for a date. What do you think you are doing but selling yourself at a job interview?

'I shan't have anything to do with the sales side.'

Rubbish.

The sales process is far more than the act of clinching the deal. If you engage a sales agent or sales representative to 'make sales' you will still be involved in the sales process. Will you never speak to customers on the telephone? Will you never handle an enquiry from a prospective customer? Will you never talk to people you meet about your business, in the hope that they might be a potential customer? Will you never have to write to a customer after the sale – a customer who might recommend you to someone else? The proprietor – like everybody else working in a business, if they did but know it – is part of a team whose job includes winning the customer. Every point of contact with a customer – whether or not it is face to face – is a test of your helpfulness, interest in the customer, warmth as a human being, a test of how you do business; a test of your business.

If you are in business, you are in the business of selling.

'I'll never make a salesperson.'

Rubbish.

Perhaps there is such a phenomenon as the born salesperson, who works from instinct, but the good news is that the techniques used by the overwhelming majority of successful professional salespeople can be learned. Their skills can be acquired and developed. Yet a scandalously high proportion of people running small businesses – and embroiled in the sales side of things – manifestly have never attempted to study the craft of salespersonship. These untrained individuals will eventually build up sufficient experience by trial and error – unless their business goes to the wall in the meantime – saying and doing what they hope to be right. And losing potential sales on their way. And never learning to maximise the sales potential.

All too often, what the hopeful, untutored individual believes to be the best thing to do, the trained professional salesperson would recognise as damaging. So the proprietor of the small shop, in the belief that they are sounding helpful, asks the customer who comes in to the shop, 'Can I help you?' This apparently innocent question puts the customer on the spot: it requires the customer to make a decision, to make a commitment. If the customer is genuinely interested in making a purchase, they will probably reply with a 'Yes'. But the customer who is unsure whether to make a purchase at all or who is merely browsing will probably back off from making a commitment. Yet these are the very persons who need to be converted to making a purchase if you are to bump up your sales figures. The correct professional approach here would be to simply engage the customer in conversation, attempting to discover the customer's wants and needs in order to match them. There will be more on this later.

You can make sales and beat the competition if you study the techniques of selling, and put them into practice. So strap yourself in: in this and the next two chapters you are to embark on an intensive mini-sales course.

You

Are you a wet blanket? Are you the character that says, 'It's bound to rain if we go.' If you heard what people said behind your back, do you think they call you negative and downbeat, or pessimistic and gloomy?

The concept of positive thinking was, until recently, regarded as 'quack' psychology, peddled by those outside the profession. In recent years, however, the techniques of positive thinking have taken on a new respectability in the UK, in the USA and in a number of Scandinavian countries. In the UK, at least one major London teaching hospital is counselling its cancer patients in the techniques. Using positive thinking will not conjure up instant 'success' in either your professional or your personal life, but many individuals go through life suffering, usually unknowingly, from the influence of negative thinking. If you are selling, a positive attitude of mind will help you live with the rejections that are part and parcel of selling. No salesperson can expect to close a sale every time, if only because not all of the prospective customers ('prospects') that they see will be genuine prospects. Perhaps some of them will, for their own reasons, have misled the salesperson into believing that they have an interest in the product, or into thinking that they are financially able to purchase, when they are not. but none of us likes to be rejected, and it is easy to interpret 'No' as being a sign of our own failing. In sales, life is a succession of challenges, each prospect representing another challenge to your skills and experience.

And remember that you are going to be wearing more than one hat, probably several, although not all at once. One hat will be labelled 'Sales Representative' and one of the others will be labelled 'Boss'. Positive thinking can help you in your role as the former, *and* help carry the manager of the small business through the ups and downs of business life.

Not all proponents of positive thinking agree as to what it encompasses, but most would probably say it promotes the following characteristics and attitudes.

- The individual is encouraged to **set goals** for him or herself. The rationale behind this is that if you take time to think about what you want, so that you know what you want, and have expressed it to yourself, you will recognise opportunities that can help you achieve these goals.

- Success is achieved by those who **keep trying**. For the salesperson this means that you must be prepared to persevere with your prospect. If the time comes when truly nothing further can be achieved with this prospect, go on to raise new leads, among whom there are bound to be prospects with whom you can succeed.

- **Jettison the 'it can't be done' mode of thinking** in yourself. Free yourself from an unnecessary handicap. Do not allow such thoughts to intrude when you strive to achieve the sales targets that you have set for the business.

181

- **Be optimistic**. The next call may be the one that results in a big order.

- **Take the initiative**. A good salesperson has an antenna for marketing information they can pick up. If you hear of somebody who might possibly be interested in your product: take the initiative, contact them.

- You have **courage**. Use it. You are not the employee of a long-established company with a pool of loyal customers: you are not merely an order taker. Propsective customers will not have heard of your fledgling enterprise. Expect to have to struggle for business. Very few buyers will actually offer you their business – you have to have the courage to ask for it.

- **Having a problem** and **encountering difficulties** is good! When you encounter the difficult prospect – the prospect who raises innumerable objections or the one who is deliberately obstructive, perhaps even aggressive – remember that with each victory over such a person you grow in wisdom and gain valuable experience.

- Each of us chooses and develops our own habits. Make a habit of **doing it now**. If you postpone calling and seeing that prospect until tomorrow, your competitor may call upon them today and close a sale.

You can control your thoughts: you can thus choose whether your attitudes in your professional and personal life will be positive or negative.

Selling yourself

Ask a salesperson what they sell and they will be only too pleased to tell you about their product. But in fact the salesperson has two things to sell: the product and the salesperson him or herself.

The situation of salesperson and prospect is one in which there exists a psychological barrier between the two parties, a barrier which the salesperson must overcome. The prospect is going to be sold something, their will is going to bend to that of the other party. Often the prospect will be wanting to resist making a purchase – either at that moment or possibly at all – wishing to avoid their will being overcome.

Even in situations in which the prospect has decided to make a purchase from some source, the encounter remains a dealing situation, very likely a situation in which two strangers are facing one another. When a customer has made the decision to buy an item they will still have matters to resolve and of which they need to be assured. What happens if things go wrong afterwards? Will they get what they have been promised? And then after the sale: have they made the right decision?

Therefore, a primary function of the salesperson is to reassure their prospect, to remove from the situation as far as is possible, any sense of tension. A vital aspect in achieving this is for the salesperson to build trust: conveying to the prospect by their credentials, what they say, the manner in which they say it, and by their body language, that they are a person on whom the prospect can depend. You need to gradually and imperceptibly reassure the prospect that they may rely on your answers, and on your opinions, and place their trust in you to the extent of giving an order to you.

One way to do this is for the salesperson to reflect the judgement and tastes of the prospect who stands in front of

183

them. After all, if the salesperson shares the same values as the prospect, the salesperson's judgement must be sound!

When opening the sales interview with your prospect spend a little while establishing a relationship with them. Convey to them that you too are a human being; they need to know that you are not a heartless con artist, nor a vending machine. Do not jump straight away into business: establish your human face and this will make it easier for the prospect to place their trust in you.

Look around at your surroundings and see if there is somethig that catches your eye that you may be able to pick up on as the subject of a brief exchange before getting down to business. It could be that something on display indicates an interest or hobby possessed by your prospect: getting them to talk about this will help them relax. Research in the USA has shown that the shaking of hands on meeting someone goes a long way to breaking down barriers between the two. It seems it is less easy to resist another when physical contact has been made with them.

The salesperson's image

It goes without saying that the salesperson should be of smart appearance, thus demonstrating respect for the customer. Unfortunately, many salespeople present an image that is too sharp; many others like to cultivate the image of a high-flying executive. This could be appropriate if your prospects are themselves affluent executives, but it is probably inappropriate for most face-to-face situations: especially where selling to the public at large it is probably better to avoid the expensive executive briefcase etc. In part, the image you wish to present to your customer will depend on what the customer is seeking from you and from your product: if you are selling investment plans your costly hand-stitched leather briefcase may signal success and be very appropriate. But the customer who is seeking to purchase insurance is probably seeking security, reliability, stability – and may not feel reassured at all by a personal appearance or demeanour that projects a glamorous or flashy image. A customer purchasing a technically complex product will be looking for technical competency and dependability: it will help if you give the appearance of a knowledgeable, practical individual, and not just a salesperson versed in the sales points of the product. Small points can help achieve this image: a technical instrument protruding from the top pocket, perhaps?

In Business History No. 5 we looked at a business whose product was burglar alarm systems and which operated largely in the domestic market selling to householders. A typical householder prospect for this product is middle class, probably middle aged or older, quite possibly retired. A customer with such a profile is less likely to be impressed by, and to take the advice and judgement of, say, a very young salesperson casually dressed. One young representative decided, after a few weeks' experience in the field, to grow a moustache and invest in a pipe! Such gimmicks can lead you into putting on an act, which can be a dangerous situation: the mask slips and the customer catches you out. It is better as far as possible to be yourself.

Smoothing the path

Your prospect needs to feel relaxed, not anxious about the situation: they are obviously less likely to commit themselves to a decision if they are in a tense frame of mind. And indeed the more relaxed your prospect is, the more likely they are to trust their own (excellent) judgement, to let their guard drop: perhaps to treat themselves and 'go for the dearer one'. It is for this reason that if there is an opportunity to inject into the meeting a social element, take it up. This is particularly so if you are dealing with the general public. If you are offered a cup of coffee, accept the offer. This will provide a natural break in the proceedings and help prevent the customer feeling they are being led inexorably to a purchase. The break in proceedings helps relax the customer and provides a natural opportunity for the salesperson to chat to them and turn to things other than the product, giving again the chance for you to sell yourself and identify with the customer; an opportunity for them to get to know you better, so they are not putting their trust in a stranger.

Selling benefits

You need to be totally familiar with your product. Only if you know all there is to know about the product can you:

- face up to questions from prospective customers with confidence;

- convey to prospective customers on air of expertise and professionalism;

- work out how to meet the customer's needs with the product;

- anticipate possible objections so as to be prepared to deal with them.

Ask yourself this question, 'How well do I know my product?'

The most valuable knowledge for the salesperson is knowledge of the **benefits** the product will confer upon customers. To explain the concept of selling benefits, sales trainers often use the example of spectacles.

A small child is instructed by his parents that he must from now on wear spectacles. An unappealing conglomeration of glass, metal and plastic, he must put the object on his nose, across his face and go about in public like this. Why? He has always been warned to be careful of glass – it is dangerous – now they want him to put it up close to his eyes!

He is told by his parents it will enable him to see better. He tries them out. They work.

By using the product, the child acquires the benefit of improved vision.

What does your product do for customers?

Note how, in our example, the consumer and the customer are not the same person. Depending on your product, a proportion of your buyers will be buying for someone else, in which case identify the benefits for your customer and the benefits for the user.

The more benefits possessed by your product, the more desirable it will be. Different buyers, however, seek different benefits. Your market research – considered in the Six-Day Action Plan – will help reveal what benefit is sought by buyers in a particular grouping. The executive may be looking for spectacles that make him look distinguished. The young person wants a fashionable look. Very likely it will not be possible for your product to appeal to all segments of the market. But other benefits will be desirable to all buyers: perhaps the spectacles you sell, unlike those of the competition, are extra comfortable.

Customers buy benefits.

> Draw up a list of the benefits your product or service will offer customers.

Why do people buy?

You need to ponder on what motivates customers to buy your product.

Again, this is a task for your market research. You have moved into probing for the broader, psychological reasons why people buy. This knowledge is pure gold. But discovering it may be like peering into a mist: the customers themselves may or may not be aware of the forces at work. The psychological motives at work upon the decision to buy may be complex. But the more accurate insight you have of what motivates your customers to buy, the more buttons you have to press . . .

Study the advertisements of successful products, especially the TV ads. Study the images projected. The TV advertisement for the car that draws up outside the Ritz Hotel, a uniformed doorman waiting respectfully upon its driver – what is the underlying desire to which the advertisement is appealing? The factors at play are age-old. You will discern in this and other advertising how use is made of the need for status, the need for self-esteem, the need for recognition, the need for security and the need for love.

In reflecting upon what makes people buy, again bear in mind that some of your customers may buy not for themselves, but on behalf of others. Is your product likely to be purchased as a gift?

In approaching the work you do upon identifying

188

customer motivation – and the benefit your product confers – bear in mind that each person has a number of roles at various stages of their lives. Notice that the motives, and benefits sought, may vary according to the role being played out at the point of purchase. You are going to be a businessperson, you may already be a spouse, perhaps you are a parent, maybe you will soon be an employer. As the hard-headed businessperson making purchases for the business you will be a very different individual from the doting parent who spends generously on your child's Christmas presents.

CHAPTER THIRTEEN

Getting orders: finding customers

You cannot make a sale to somebody who has never heard of you. Your prospective customer may hear of you for the first time when you attempt to make the sale, but it is much easier to make a sale if you are already known to the potential buyer. From whom the customer is buying can be just as important as what the customer is buying. The reputation of the supplier, how long they have been established, is relevant to the ability of the customer to rely on the supplier's claims for the product, the quality of the product and the after-sales service. But nobody has ever heard of your brand-new little business. So from the date of its birth – and even before – you must tell the world of its existence. Just like Cadbury's or Sony or Ford or Coca-Cola. Yes, you might learn of their existence when you buy their product, when you go into the shop and see the product that bears their name, but before you ever get to that stage these companies will have spent millions of pounds and dollars and yen on promoting their name and existence to the world at large. You hear of them when you discover that the charity event you are attending is sponsored by them, or when you read in the newspapers or trade journal that they have won a big new order, or when their name is caught by the television camera at the sporting event they are helping to sponsor. Much of this activity is the work of their public relations departments: on a scaled-down basis your public relations department – you – can do the same thing.

It is, of course, possible for you to use the services of a public relations consultancy or agency, although whether the likely income to be generated by your part-time activities will justify the expenditure on their professional fees is a question for only you to answer. But if you are capable of running your own business you are capable of acquiring and using the basic techniques of PR.

Getting known

TELL EVERYBODY

Let everyone know that you are about to set up in business and what you will be doing. When you have launched off, tell them you are now trading. Tell your friends, relatives, workmates, neighbours, the person behind the counter at your corner shop. Whenever you find yourself in conversation with anybody, get into the habit of asking yourself, 'Can I tell this person about my business?'

I have been surprised to learn how many newcomers to business are afraid to trumpet to the world that they are in business. Very often this stems from lack of confidence, but probably also you are unaccustomed to promoting yourself and your activities. Overcome such inhibitions. In my experience your very first orders can come from such word-of-mouth promotion, from personal contacts. Perhaps your neighbour is not in the market for your product, but his brother is a potential customer for one, and it just so happens he visits your neighbour the day after you've been talking about it to him. Tell enough people and someone somewhere will prove to be a potential customer – or will turn up one for you. Naturally you will have had printed some professional-looking business cards to hand out, and very few businesses indeed cannot benefit from the use of a sales leaflet telling the world about their product or service.

Come up with ways in which your specific business operations would give you the chance to talk to people and tell them what you are doing. For example, in Business History No. 5 we heard what befell Anne Y on her first excursion into business, the setting up of a burglar alarm company. When the day came to install the system, Anne would knock upon the doors of all the houses within hearing distance of the alarm bell, ostensibly to warn the householder that the alarm bell would be ringing for test purposes and that they should not act upon it. This was an example of good public relations, defusing the potential anxiety and annoyance of neighbours suffering the noise of an unexpected alarm bell. But it served also as an opportunity to tell others who the company was and what it was doing; an opportunity also for a potential customer to discover how pleasant and helpful was the company's representative; and for that representative to plant in the neighbour's mind the thought that they also should consider installing a burglar alarm: after all, to whom will the frustrated burglar turn their attentions when deterred by the alarm from breaking in next door?

EMBLAZON YOUR NAME

With small-scale operations the opportunities for emblazoning your name and/or logo on company property are limited, but your mode of transport can provide you with publicity at minimal outlay. If you will be using a van, merely because it is elderly does not mean it should be tatty. Build into your start-up costs the price of a respray to cover rust, dents and a previous owner's signwriting. The colour of your van, and any signwriting, will have to fit in with the image of your business and its product, but make it eye-catching and attractive. Here is an opportunity to tell others of your existence while waiting in the queue at the traffic-lights. If you are calling on customers at home, here is your opportunity to say who you are and what you do to the person behind the twitching curtain in the house opposite.

If you don't need a van, or funds won't run to the cost and the family car will be doubling up, take advantage of inexpensive self-adhesive signs that fit on the doors. Look for suppliers in *Yellow Pages* or the *Exchange and Mart.*

Is your business one where you and others working with you can arrive dressed in company workwear sporting your business name and logo? If your service involves manual operations you will also look more professional and efficient if you arrive dressed in appropriate workwear.

NEWSPAPERS AND MAGAZINES

Both in-house PR departments and PR consultants make routine use of press releases to gain coverage in the news columns rather than by paid-for advertising. An item in the newspaper about your business can have more impact than an advertisement by a competitor for which they have paid. We all approach advertising with a certain degree of scepticism; by contrast, our defences are lowered when we read in the newspaper of the success of a local business that has secured a huge order for its product.

If you have no experience of securing coverage in newspapers, magazines and trade journals you may be pleasantly surprised how easily this can be achieved. This is partly because newspapers and magazines have to cover the space with print and are in need of items to write about, but

193

it is also because much of the material is fed to them by professional PR people who have this insider knowledge: first, the easier you make it for a journalist to use your material, the more likely it is that they will do so; secondly, the more likely it is you will read about yourself and your business if it is genuinely of interest to readers. In practice, because of the need to fill up column inches some of the material that finds its way into the press is in reality of little interest to most readers; an example is the tantalising news that Mr Smith has been appointed the new area sub-manager, north-eastern division, distribution operations, for X Limited. This has probably found its way in because the journalist who has made use of it is fed material regularly by the PR department concerned and simply routinely publishes it. You should aim to tell the press about something newsworthy that has what the professionals call human interest.

It is of interest to readers of the local press that a new business has been set up in their area, since this is a new source of a product or service for them, but realistically the fact that Mrs Jones has set up a new ironing service at Oglander Road will struggle to find its way into the news columns. But you can add to its newsworthy value by having a launch day. Invite someone who has some sort of claim to fame – a local councillor, the deputy mayor, the chair of the local chamber of commerce – to be guest of honour at an opening ceremony for your launch-off. Give advance notice in your press release and tell the local paper that there will be photo opportunities. You will need something for your guest to be doing when they pose before the camera: perhaps cutting a ribbon, or examining the details of your first contract, or shaking hands in congratulations. In case the press photographer does not turn up, arrange for your own photographer to be present. Ask around and you will turn up a keen amateur photographer who does weddings in their spare time and is quite capable of producing photographs that you can send off after the event to other newspapers and trade journals.

If you do not know how to go about devising a press release, you are about to acquire a most useful business skill. . . .

Layout of press release
Bear in mind the following pointers:

- a margin of a minimum of 1in at the top and on either side of the page, and 1.5in at the foot;

- no blank line between paragraphs;

- typing double spaced;

- indent paragraphs, say five spaces – but not the opening paragraph;

- at the end of the first page on a fresh line type 'more' on the right-hand side;

- do not carry a paragraph over on to a second page;

- on the last page on a fresh line type 'ends';

- give a reasonably accurate word count in the covering letter;

- if more than one page, staple pages together;

- type on one side only of A4 paper;

- include a headline at the top but do not underline this (underlining is used by the journalist as an instruction to the printers).

Include, in either your covering letter or the release, the name and phone number of the person who can be contacted for further information.

To make life easier for the busy journalist you must strive to write your press releases so they need the minimum of alteration. Study the style of writing in the paper or journal you are aiming at and write your release as close as you can to that style. When analysing the style of local newspapers and popular journals you will see that paragraphs are short and punchy. Keep your sentences short also.

Many items in the press convey the impression that an individual has spoken directly to the reporter. You may be surprised to learn that this is the work of a knowledgeable PR consultant who has included in the release a direct quotation. '"An order of this size means that we will be taking on extra staff," said Mr Hogan.' This gives more immediacy and life to the item.

An item about a big new order or taking on staff or offering some new facility locally will publicise your business without the item being too obviously a simple plug, which the paper is unlikely to use.

Ask some friends to read over what you have written to check that the meaning is clear. Don't use a long word if a short word will suffice. Don't use more words than you have to: re-read it yourself asking whether there are any words that could be deleted without altering the meaning. For example, in that preceding sentence did I really need the word 'any'? If you include a quote say it aloud to yourself to make sure it sounds authentic.

RADIO ... AND TV?

Like your local newspaper, your local radio station has to fill up space. Here you will be aiming either to get a mention over the airspace or, better still, an interview. In either case your first shot could be in the form of a news release, followed up by a phone call. If they ask you to come along to the studio and you've never done an interview before, you may be in for a few surprises. If you are new to this game you will presume that before the broadcast the presenter will go over with you in outline what they will be saying to you and the questions they will be putting. On each occasion that I have been on local radio the busy presenter has not had time to do this. The first time I got caught out. The second time I made sure that while a record was being played I checked up on what questions I would be asked.

You may be surprised by the tone of the presenter's questioning: the questions may come across as almost aggressive. But the presenter is not there just to let you give a straightforward plug for your product or service, telling the world for free how wonderful it is – this has got to be more than just an advertisement. So expect the interview to be challenging and go over in your mind beforehand what questions the presenter might ask you and map out your answers. Include awkward questions that might be asked.

If the thought of such public speaking gives you butterflies in your tummy and you are convinced you are going to make a mess of it . . . then do it as often as you can! Public speaking is a superb example of something which improves with practice. So. . . .

SPEAKING IN PUBLIC

Offer to give a talk to local organisations. The parish newsletter is a source of information as to which groups exist locally and who to contact. For example, when Anne set up her burglar alarm business she offered to speak to local groups about security in the home, taking the opportunity, of course, to demonstrate her company's system. To be successful at this you've got to offer your potential audience something useful and interesting that they will want to hear. Anne directed her activities at women's groups, slanting her talk to security for the woman in the home and on the street.

Here are the basics of public speaking.

Don't

- have a few drinks beforehand;

- be late;

- talk to the window;

- read aloud a prepared speech;

- distract your audience with a habit;

- try to be a stand-up comedian;

- forget to explain the jargon.

You can try out your opening and some extracts in front of a friend, asking them to watch out in particular for habits you may have that you are not aware of. Do you rub your nose? Do you play with your pen? Do you unconsciously pull funny faces?

Do

- find out about your audience beforehand;

- be prepared;

- check in the mirror before you go in;

- smile;

- structure what you are going to say;

- vary your rate of speech;

- vary your volume.

A check in the mirror might reveal the remnants on your face of sausage roll from the welcoming buffet beforehand or that your trouser flies are undone.

People like to know where they are going and they like things broken down into digestible chunks. So if you are going to look at a number of matters tell them how many beforehand and tell them what number you are at as you go through.

RECOMMENDATIONS

Someone who knows you are in business might pass on your name to a friend who is looking for your product or service. Of course, to pass on your name they've got to know you're in business, which is what this section is all about. The nicest business of all comes when a *customer* passes on your name. Such recommended business has cost you nothing in advertising fees and yet can be the easiest sale to make.

But why should your customers recommend you? Because you have a good product. A good product encompasses not just the physical, tangible item that you sell. It includes the service that surrounds it. This brings us to two buzz words of modern business:

QUALITY SERVICE

There isn't universal agreement as to what this expression contemplates. The common definition is that you provide quality service when your business provides the customer with that to which they are entitled. To me, this is the *minimum* service which the customer can expect. In my own business the definition of quality service I strive for is

> *giving the customer more than they expect*

Going that extra distance ... Giving the customer that little bit more than a competitor would give them.

You have no better opportunity of putting this philosophy into practice than when something goes wrong. A testing test of quality service is when your customer has a complaint. Tell them you are sorry of course – and mean it – then put it right as soon as you possibly can. Think of some way in which you can go the extra mile. If what went wrong was of any import *to the customer* make a gesture: perhaps offer some small gift with your compliments. All of this shows that you have grasped the essential prerequisite of customer satisfaction: that you are able to put yourself in the shoes of your customer, to see things from their point of view, not just from the point of view of the business. This last sentence is so vital I suggest you read it again.

The need for excellence in customer relations pushed many firms in the 1980s into installing customer service training for staff, for which, as customers, we have much to be thankful. But small businesses don't have in-house customer service training courses and most of them don't send their staff on public courses which are open to them. Do you think that tradespeople you deal with, such as the plumber or electrician or decorater running their own small business, have been on customer service courses?

Here is your own in-house micro quality service course.

Quality service
Start your training by thinking of bad examples of service that you have received as a customer. Analyse what was wrong. Draw up a list of these and add to it from time to time – for example when you are on the receiving end of poor service yourself. Head this document 'Examples of what I will not do in my business' and keep it in your in-tray: in that way you will come across it every so often. When you do, make sure you re-read it to remind yourself of its valuable contents.

Make a copy of the following list and put it with your sheet of common examples of poor service.

IN RUNNING MY BUSINESS I WILL NOT:

- turn up late without ringing beforehand to say that I will not be on time and why this is so

- fail to turn up at all without any explanation

- fail to turn up at all without any explanation on the appointed day and then simply turn up out of the blue on another day

- sound bored

- send different goods without explanation

- fail to write/phone and say the goods will be delayed

- give inferior service to a person because of the colour of their skin, or because of their youth, or because of their manner of dress, or because of their accent

---

Treat all customers and potential customers as important people. They are important people – to your business and to themselves. And anyway, it's a nice thing to do.

Here is another list for you to copy and add to your in-tray.

I will not say any of the following things in the course of running my business:

'I've no idea, mate.'

'Yes, dear?'

'We don't do that – my assistant shouldn't have said that we could.'

'No, we changed our opening hours, what's on the leaflet is wrong.'

Opposite is a word-for-word transcript of a telephone conversation I endured recently – it's useful to have an answering machine that records conversations as well as messages – when trying to find a supplier of a garden shed:

Telephone rings 11 times before it is answered.

Moron: Hello.

Me: Hello?

Moron: Hello.

Me: Is that Moron's Sectional Buildings?

Moron: Yes.

Me: Good morning.

SILENCE

Me: I was wondering if you are open today.

Moron: Well obviously or I wouldn't be here to answer the phone.

Surprised silence at my end.

Me: Can you tell me what time you close, please?

Moron: We're open until round about lunchtime.

Me: Well can you be a bit more precise. What's round about lunchtime mean?

Moron: If we have only a few customers we shut.

Pause

Me: Well how am I supposed to know whether you are open or not — it's a half-hour journey for me to come to you.

Moron: It's underneath the counter.

Me: Sorry?

Moron: I was talking to somebody else.

Loud crashing noise . . .

At this point we were cut off. Re-read this example and make a list of the failings demonstrated by the person who was representing the business on the telephone.

Of course not all customers know how to conduct themselves properly. In my experience a tiny percentage, perhaps 2 per cent are unreasonable, and a microscopic percentage, perhaps 0.002 per cent, are potty. When you have been in business long enough you will learn to spot early the signs when it comes to the latter and will politely and quickly withdraw. As regards the rude customer, there may be an explanation for their behaviour which is not known to you: for example your misdoings may be the third incident of bad service the customer has received this week. This does not justify their rudeness but as they are human it would help to explain it. Personally I will never take rudeness from a customer beyond an initial momentary lapse. The arrogant person in the shop who treats staff in a contemptuous fashion makes me squirm with embarrassment: I wouldn't put up with that and nor should you. We don't need their money that much and by putting up with them you encourage such behaviour.

All that has just been said about quality in your business is of gold-plated importance when your product is itself a service.

The selling of services

Earlier the observation was made in passing that it is probably easier to set up a business where your product is a service. This is partly because very often the start-up costs are lower: if your product is something you have invented you will have to invest in production facilities; if it is something you are buying in you may be required by your supplier to invest in heavy stocks or a commitment to take stock at regular intervals. It is no wonder that in so many areas of high unemployment there are a large number of window cleaners! Their small investment in little more than a bucket, sponge and leather is an example of how low start-up costs for service-based businesses attract numerous entrants – and lead to more intensive price competition.

If your product is to be a service then you also face this truth: the selling of a service presents additional hurdles and requires particular skills.

Insurance, transport, entertainment, recreation, education, consultancy, design, research, investment, cleaning and maintenance, are all service-based businesses. They could make a business for you. But if you set up in any of these you will have no tangible product. Your prospective customers can't see the holiday you are endeavouring to sell them. You can show them pictures of the sea but they can't see the sea or put their fingers in it. This makes it more difficult for your potential buyer to assess quality. And with an intangible product it is more difficult for your prospect to judge the value of what they are getting. Allow your prospect to try out a lawnmower and they can see immediately some of the benefits they will receive for their investment – but the benefits they will receive from the insurance policy you are trying to sell are less apparent. All of this makes it necessary for the prospective customer to place greater reliance on what the suppliers tell them they will receive; they must place in the suppliers greater trust. This in turn places a greater burden on the suppliers' salesperson. Of course the reputation of the business for integrity and proper dealing will facilitate the placing of the customer's trust – but your business is a new business which has not yet built up such a reputation. So for you, even more than for your established competitors, your salesperson must radiate integrity, solidity, reliability, consistency.

The successful sale of a service requires the customer to take a large dose of T and C: trust and confidence. Nurture it by demeanour, appearance, professionalism, knowledge. You can get the order. Remember, every business whose product is a service had to get order number one.

Leads

The member of the public making a purchase in a retail shop probably thinks that nearly all sales are made in such a way. The customer who buys something in a shop does not stop to consider how that item had first to be sold *to* the shop, perhaps by a wholesaler, who in turn had bought from a manufacturer, who had perhaps bought raw materials from an importer.

The salesperson who works in a shop selling over the counter employs the same basic skills as the salesperson who sells to industry and commerce, but a major difference in the two types of salesperson is that the one operating in the shop has a stream of prospective customers coming into the store. By doing so, the prospective customer is indicating an interest in the products the shop offers. But for other salespeople – those who sell to industry, or to the wholesale trade, or to manufacturing, or even to consumers buying at home – there will be a greater seeking out of potential customers. Of course, the shop must – just like your business – make its presence and its wares known, in this case in order to attract potential buyers through the doors. But the salesperson who is not operating in a retail shop may have to go out and *hunt* for prospective customers, the prospects. Such a person needs to identify who these prospects are, to induce them to do something to indicate their interest in the product, just as the customer in the shop indicates an interest by stepping over the threshold. When this indication of interest has been given, the salesperson has a 'lead' to follow.

One or more of these lead-raising methods may be suitable for your business.

ADVERTISING

For the newcomer to business, this is usually the most obvious and first thought for getting business. An advertising agency will do all the work for you, but in all likelihood their fees would not fit into the budget of your mini-business. That friendly voice selling newspaper advertising will probably make some suggestions to help you avoid pitfalls; after all, they want the advertising to work – but their job is to sell you advertising space, so expect them to try to sweep you along, agreeing to more than you need. An astonishingly high proportion of small businesses are quite happy to devise their own advertisements; but an amateurish effort without knowledge of the copywriter's basic techniques stands a good chance of being of nil effect – or at best, less effective, reducing the value of the advertising. You will find the absolute fundamentals in the subsection on advertising later in this chapter.

DROP LEAFLETS

The term applies to leaflets delivered door to door. Leaflets can, of course, be inserted loose into magazines or mailed to prospective customers: drop leaflets are particularly suitable where the prospect is the average householder. They are less suitable where the product is one for industry or commerce, although the method can be used where there is a concentration of prospective customers in a particular area, such as an industrial estate.

The advantages of drop leaflets include the following.

- A specific area can be targeted. This may be a necessity where you are aiming for a particular market, say middle-income homeowners, and it is necessary to avoid blanket coverage.

- Drop leaflets can give you greater control over the flow of leads. Experience will tell you the number of leaflets that have to be put out on average over a given period of time to produce X number of leads. The quantities of leaflets going out can be adjusted to, hopefully, produce a regular number of leads coming in, providing you with sufficient business, but only at a rate of calls that you can comfortably handle.

To encourage the person who picks up the leaflet from the mat to respond, he or she must receive the promise of something. Offer something attractive: the more attractive it is the more likely the person is to send back the leaflet. This something could be a free colour brochure, or a demonstration, or a free sample.

This leads to the question as to whether your drop leaflet should let the prospective customer know that a salesperson will be calling if they respond. With the general public, it is common not to do so. Drop leaflets, or indeed other forms of advertising to the public, that hold out the prospect of a salesperson calling have a dramatically lower reply rate – although it may be that the quality of replies is better, resulting in improved conversion rates.

MAILSHOTS

This is a method of reaching a closely defined target market. List brokers sell names and addresses of individuals and businesses whose previous purchases indicate that your product is likely to be of interest to them.

CANVASSERS

Canvassers who call in person (as opposed to telephone canvassers) are more usually found in sales operations selling direct to the public, home improvements for example. You will need gritty determination to accept endless rebuffs – and worse – from angry householders who have left the meal table to answer the door to a canvasser! But if you can stomach it and can acquire the skills you will always be able to go out and seek business. Novices soon learn the lesson that some members of the public will allow the canvasser to log their name and address as an interested party, simply in order to get rid of the canvasser: the quality of leads raised in this manner can be poor.

EXHIBITIONS AND TRADE SHOWS

Exhibiting at a trade show can be costly, not merely in terms of the rental costs, but taking into account the labour needed to attend a stand during the long hours of an exhibition day. Many companies, especially larger ones, expend considerable sums of money on their stands and it may be difficult for the small business with limited funds to stand out from the competition. You may be able to attract sufficient interest to make it worth your while if your product is new or unusual. The flip side of this is that you may end up deluged with leads which then have to be dealt with before they go cold: and you have taken three days' holiday entitlement from your regular job to attend the exhibition, and are due back in the office tomorrow.

Prospecting

What we have looked at so far are ways of inducing prospective customers to themselves indicate their interest in your product, but it is possible to detect their likely interest in some other way. For the hungry salesperson other methods of hunting out prospects include these.

THE PRESS

Local newspapers can be a particular source of information. The sort of item you can be looking out for includes companies announcing expansion or winning a contract, news of a branch that is opening and details of new appointments, such as a new buyer you could approach.

TRADE DIRECTORIES

These are held by or obtainable through the reference section of public libraries – they are expensive to purchase. Most trade directories provide detailed information which will arm you, the salesperson, with knowledge of the prospective customer and increased credibility when approaching them. Useful info that can be gained includes names of directors, number of employees, turnover, products and the company's markets.

TELEPHONE CANVASSING

Telephone canvassing is not the same thing as telephone sales. The latter is where the salesperson endeavours to conclude a sale on the telephone: a method particularly suited to where the prospect does not need to see the product, either because it can be adequately described or because it is familiar to them. Telephone canvassing is where the canvasser endeavours to sell the customer an appointment at which a sales presentation will be made.

In selling to industry and commerce, where you will be endeavouring to contact the official buyer, you can expect to come up against a secretary instructed to keep the buyer undisturbed by sales reps. The golden rule is to treat the secretary with courtesy and politeness – while being firm.

EXISTING CUSTOMERS

Try asking them: 'What would I have to do for you to give me more business?'

RECOMMENDATIONS

You can do more than merely hope that, in the light of the quality of your product and service, satisfied customers will pass on your name: discreetly implant in their minds the idea that they might very kindly recommend you and your products to other people. Mention, for example, that much of your work comes from personal recommendations; you may be pleasantly surprised by the percentage of customers who then respond, 'Well I shall certainly recommend you.'

Going further, your product or service may lend itself to a 'Recommend A Friend' scheme. Supply customers with a leaflet offering a gift or cash as a thank you for passing on your name to a friend or relative who makes a purchase. Include with the leaflet a coupon for the customer to complete with the name and address of their friend. Such a scheme can be particularly productive where your product is a highly visible purchase, such as a new carpet, that will be noticed and admired by your customer's acquaintances.

REFERRALS

This is a method of prospecting that has been long used in the insurance business: the salesperson asks somebody to suggest the names of others who might be interested in the product. This is not the same strategy as asking for a recommendation: you can put this request to friends and relatives who are not in the market for your product, but who will help you by suggesting the names of others who might be. And try out such a request on the potential customer you didn't convert to a sale: frame your approach along the lines that if the product wasn't suitable for their particular circumstances, it may well suit X. From an unsuccessful presentation you can salvage something that could be valuable.

Advertising

For most small businesses advertising will play a large part in arousing the interest of prospective customers, especially during the early days. But drafting the ad – getting the layout and text right – can seem a headache.

The starting point is to choose the right media to match your target market. Newspaper advertising will give blanket coverage suitable only if your product is one directed at a sufficient proportion of general readers. Magazines and journals, especially trade journals, will enable you to target your advertising at a particular market. Thus, if your product is something sold only to hospitals and doctors, it would be uneconomic to advertise in popular newspapers as opposed to medical journals.

Two essentials that must be borne in mind when drafting an ad:

- the ad must, above all else, attract attention to itself;

- the ad must urge the reader to respond to it.

Advertising professionals call the text in an advertisement the *copy*. We saw earlier how customers buy benefits: the copy for your advertisement must be about what the product does for prospective customers, the benefits it has for them. In drafting your copy draw upon the list of benefits you have compiled for your product. Place emphasis on those benefits that are exclusive to you, or that are new, or that represent a step forward in your field.

Very likely your ad will sit among a mass of other competing advertisements and text: it has only moments to seize the reader's attention. You will need a *headline*, which must capture the attention of the reader.

In drafting your copy, ask yourself: what is my target market? Or put another way, who am I talking to?

Make sure your copy tells the readers what you want them to do, such as fill in and return the enquiry coupon.

The most successful words used by advertising copywriters are of course 'free' and 'new'. Their pulling power is undeniable – but don't overdo them!

213

CHAPTER FOURTEEN

Getting orders: the sales presentation

The popular stereotype image of a salesperson is of a fast-talking individual pressurising the poor customer into buying something they do not want. Naturally, this is not how you will conduct business.

But once your business is up and running, and you are making sales, pause and look in the mirror: are you sure your customers would not recognise you if they heard this description? The most common failing of people in sales is simply that they are seduced into talking too much.

The need to listen

The modern professional approach to sales is not that of the fast-talking con artist. Today's more sophisticated sales-person is acutely aware of the need to

listen.

The knowledgeable salesperson listens to what the cust-omers have to say and reads their body language. The

214

enduring small business is not out to con everybody into buying its product whether they need it or not and whether it suits their needs or not. The person achieving its sales listens to what the prospects say in order to discover what are the benefits they could derive from the product.

If you can get the customer to talk you can learn from them what are their needs and what are their desires. A customer's needs are those things which they must have, such as food; a customer's desires are those things which the particular customer may like to have, such as status. By listening to what your prospective customers say, discovering their needs and desires, you can match these to the benefits that your product offers. You can demonstrate to the customer that your product offers what it is that they wish to receive from it. But how can you do this if you do not know what it is that the customer wishes to obtain from their purchase?

A small business can learn from a big business, and Anne, the proprietor of the small burglar alarm business, learned a great deal from a friend who had worked for three years for an established alarm company, one that had more than a dozen sales reps. The friend's product boasted numerous benefits and the company was the market leader in the region. This company's representatives were trained to listen carefully to what their prospective customers were saying.

Not all of the product's benefits will be sought by every customer. The prospective customer for a burglar alarm who mentions in passing that 'my sister bought a burglar alarm and it wasn't reliable' is clearly looking for a system which will offer reliability. The customer who greets the representative by saying, 'You are lucky to catch us in at the weekend because we go away most weekends in our caravan' is revealing unwittingly a demonstrable need for a security system for premises which are frequently left unattended. Later, the representative can point out to the customer that their premises are vulnerable to a prospective intruder who has observed the customer's regular habit of going away at weekends.

You cannot rely on your customers giving you voluntarily all the information that you require: you may need to do some probing to elicit the customer's needs and desires. It may be necessary to ask questions, perhaps framed in an apparently innocent fashion, to bring out information that will point you to the benefits that your customer will receive from the product. Endeavour to induce a situation where the customer feels able to converse with you: a reason for accepting that cup of coffee mentioned earlier.

Assessing your customer

The salesperson has to size up their customer. They will be doing this instinctively when they meet a Prospect, and will have begun to make judgements about the type of person the customer is even before they have met. Thus, the salesperson selling direct to the customer in the home may be able to make provisional judgements from the type of house the customer has, or even, before the visit, from the customer's address. Where the prospective customer has indicated an interest in the product (as opposed to the salesperson cold calling), the nature of the product itself will say something about the customer: the seller of burglar alarm systems is likely to find someone interested in alarms to be a security-minded, prudent individual. An awareness of the type of person you are likely to be dealing with will provide you with some clues as to the likely benefits they will be looking for.

The experienced salesperson, however, is always

prepared on meeting a Prospect to rapidly reassess any provisional pre-meeting judgements. They may discover that a Prospect has not the slightest interest in or desire to own a burglar alarm system: it is a requirement forced upon the customer by their insurers.

Profiles of customers for your particular trade are an example of valuable information you can pick up from published market research. We looked at sources of such information in the Action Plan.

Handling objections

Every salesperson faces numerous objections to purchasing their product.

You should try to make your replies to objections:

- concise;

- flexible; and

- polite.

Always give your prospect the impression that you are listening carefully to the point they are making. Pause slightly before replying so that your prospect does not gain the impression that you are just glibly replying with the standard response. Depending on the circumstances, it may be appropriate to agree to some extent with your prospect's objection, but then to deal with it in such a way that the objection does not retain validity in this particular case.

> List every possible objection you can think of to your product or service, then devise a credible answer to each.
>
> Add to your list from time to time as you encounter further objections.

PRICE

It is a fact of life that price is the most common objection to the making of a purchase.

Much can be done to forestall objections to price by building up the customer's expectations that price will be high. The higher the price the customer is expecting, the more reasonable the actual price will appear when it is revealed!

In Business History No. 6 we looked at a small business supplying loose covers for furniture. You will recall that the proprietor, Dennis, had been a professional salesman before taking early retirement. He had several years' experience of selling direct to customers in the home. Average price for a set of made-to-measure loose covers was in the range of £300 – £400, not far short of the price at which it was possible to buy a new suite of furniture, though not one of the best quality. Dennis anticipated that price was likely to be a common objection: how could Dennis prepare the customer so that the information as to price was received in a favourable state of mind?

Drawing on his experience and sales training, one tactic Dennis chose was to ensure that it took him a considerable time to work out the price for the customer. This tactic helps convey to the customer the impression that a lot of work will be involved in the job itself. This technique cannot be used where there is a standard price, but is particularly suited to work involving labour and for which the price has to be individually calculated. If this applies to your business, then ostentatiously jot down figures, draw rough diagrams, add up figures and punch away on your calculator. As your customer watches this process, the more his anxiety about the price grows, so the actual price may come as a pleasant surprise.

A further tactic to use when quoting price is to break it down into various components, as opposed to giving a straightforward price for the whole job. It will help to make the price seem more reasonable if you itemise what the customer is getting and show how the price is built up. In the case of loose covers, Dennis found that a good percentage of customers expected their set of covers to have frills around the bottom and edging of some sort around the cushions. Dennis spelt out these items separately and gave a price for each of them, helping to convey the impression that the customer was receiving a number of items, not just one, in return for their outlay.

We have probably all at some time witnessed use made of the technique of conveying to the customer the impression that a lot of work or materials are involved: the garage mechanic for example who, asked to estimate the cost of repairs, purses his or her lips. Today's consumer may regard this example as a rather crude method of attempting to build price expectation: you will endeavour to introduce price expectation in a more innocuous manner. With Fencraft Covers, Dennis stood back to admire the roominess of the customer's suite, the customer agreeing what a lovely, big, roomy suite of furniture it was. Later, when pricing, Dennis mentioned that while it is lovely to have a roomy suite, the trouble is of course that it uses up a great deal of fabric, making this observation as he works out the price figure in front of the customer.

We saw in our Action Plan that for the customer price is an indicator of quality: the higher the price, the better the quality. This expectation can be used by the salesperson: objections to price can receive the reaction, 'But of course – what do you expect? The price reflects the quality.'

Some customers want a really high price: it signals exclusivity and demonstrates to their acquaintances how well off financially they are.

But perhaps your little business will not be operating in such a market!

Closing the deal

Closing the deal – going for the order – requires a bit of courage: you will be afraid of rejection.

Knowing – and having used to good effect in the past – some sales techniques for closing will bolster your confidence.

What you must do is *lead* the customer up to the deal. Here are some proven closing techniques.

THE ALTERNATIVE CLOSE

You ask a question which gives your prospect an alternative. The prospect's mind focuses upon which alternative to choose. The nature of the question you put is such that by opting for one of the alternatives, the prospect is making a commitment himself. Example: 'Would you like delivery before you go on holiday or after you come back?'

THE 'INCH AT A TIME' CLOSE

Here you ask a series of questions. Each relates to some detail of the transaction. Your prospect agrees with each detail in turn. Step by step you cover all the details of the deal.

You have broken down the decision – the decision to purchase – into small decisions, each individually far easier to take. Their cumulative effect is that an order has crept up on the prospect.

TURN ROUND AN OBJECTION

An objection may turn out to be your best ally. The stronger the objection appears to be, the better!

Demolish the objection.

Then turn to your impressed prospect: you have answered the objection to their complete satisfaction: now it would be unreasonable to refuse an order.

THE SUMMARY CLOSE

Here you summarise briefly the benefits which you have agreed with the prospect during your presentation: there is simply nothing left to be dealt with. With all those benefits, surely they must place an order!

THE FEAR CLOSE

A popular technique. You emphasise the benefits that will be *lost* if the prospect does not go ahead. This often comes in the form of the special offer with a time limit.

THE ASSUMPTIVE CLOSE

You prompt your prospect into talking about the product or service as if they have already decided they are going to have it.

Experience is needed to develop the technique, *but* if you are apprehensive about going for the close, fearful of losing the sale, this gentler approach could be for you. This is a subtle approach: take pleasure in developing and using the skills demanded.

Here is an example of this powerful closing technique in action: the assumptive close seemed likely to Anne Y to lend itself to sales of burglar alarms. As we saw, Anne sold her small business, since when it has continued to grow. The assumptive close remains the company's preferred approach and its three sales representatives are schooled in the techniques. Anne's business markets a system based on the concept of movement detection. The movement of an intruder within the protected area is picked up by an ultrasonic transmitter termed the detector head. The detector head transmits and receives signals, imperceptible to the human ear, the frequency of which is disturbed by a given level of movement. Benefits of the system include being more suitable for use in the home, because the amount of visible wiring is reduced, and it can be cheaper than conventional systems thanks to the reduction of labour involved in installation. For the average home two detector heads provide adequate coverage.

On receipt of an enquiry the company posts sales literature to the prospect. A covering letter with the literature mentions that the company's security consultant will call upon the prospect to give a free, no-obligation security survey. Within two or three days the security consultant – in the early days it was always Anne – makes the call, armed with a functioning sample system to demonstrate to the prospect.

The sales presentation is directed at acclimatising the prospect to the idea of having and using a burglar alarm system. The consultant involves the prospect in doing things, or agreeing with statements, so that without realising it, the prospect is beginning to talk as if they are having a burglar alarm system. The consultant induces the prospect into suggesting how the system would work in their house. The consultant coaxes the prospect into suggesting the most suitable point to locate the detector head. The consultant suggests that the detector head be located in X position, but then prompts the prospect into suggesting Y position. The consultant achieves this by going across to Y position and gazing at it thoughtfully in silence for some time, as if wondering whether that would be a more suitable location.

Having 'suggested' Y position, the prospect can then be encouraged into pointing out how well this would work. The prospect can be prompted by appropriate questions from the consultant to point out how, in the position they have suggested intruders will be picked up by the detector as soon as they climb through a rear window, or wherever.

The process at work here is triply effective: the prospect is becoming acclimatised to the idea of having the product, plus at the same time the benefits are brought out, plus the benefits are brought out by the prospect him or herself! Your prospective customer is going to be more impressed with the truth of a statement as to the benefits of your product when the statement has been made by the prospect him or herself!

CHAPTER FIFTEEN

Consumer law

In Chapter 11 we looked at the law of contract, an area of law that impinges enormously on the daily life of a business. An appreciation of contract law is a prerequisite for an understanding of much of consumer law, another area of law to which the business must be alert.

This book offers a taste of a range of subjects, acquaintance with which will increase the likelihood of business success and I hope very much that your appetite has been whetted, and that you will go on to deepen your knowledge in each area. The ever-pervasive character of law – it touches upon the activities of the business at every turn – and the growth in the regulation of business activities makes it a non-optional study for those who take seriously the obligations imposed on us. Once you are in business this will be underlined for you as you deal with today's heightened customer expectations and awareness of legal rights. But while law is a vital study, and often an absorbing subject, most of us find it can be intellectually demanding. My experience is that it is more digestible taken in small servings, with time between for what has gone before to settle.

Thus it is that we now return to law.

The term consumer law is an umbrella title for a diversity of legal provisions whose objective is the protection of those who buy goods or services. As with contract law, given the breadth and depth of the law, our objective here must be to give you an *awareness* of the subject, highlighting the principles of provisions which are likely to be most relevant to the small business.

As we shall see, much of the law that regulates buying and selling differentiates between customers who are 'consumers' and customers who are themselves in business. For most purposes, the major characteristic of a consumer is that they are someone who does not buy in the course of a business. The distinction is an important one since, in a non-consumer transaction, it *may* be possible for the supplier of goods or services to exclude or restrict some of the principal legal obligations placed upon them.

Which portions of the law are most relevant to your business depends very much upon whether you are in the business of selling goods or in the business of supplying services.

Sale of goods

If your business sells goods, then your sales are subject to the Sale of Goods Act 1979. In a contract for the sale of goods, and indeed in any type of contract, that which the parties agree between them are the *terms of the contract*. Turning to the illustration we used in Chapter 11 on contract law, in a sale by the part-time car trader he will agree with his customer such matters as the price, the date of delivery and how payment is to be made. Matters specifically agreed between the parties are known as *express terms*, but the law also inserts in the contract terms which the parties have not expressly agreed. These *implied terms* can sometimes be ousted by the parties, but in other instances they remain a part of the contract whether or not both parties wish it. In practice, since the term is more often imposed for the protection of the buyer, it will be the seller who wishes to push out of the agreement a term that Parliament has inserted, removing an obligation placed upon the seller. It is the device of the implied contract term that is the principle vehicle of consumer protection.

The major terms implied by the Sale of Goods Act for the protection of buyers are:

- a term that where goods have been sold by description, the goods will correspond with that description;

- a term requiring the goods to be of 'merchantable quality';

- where the buyer wants the goods for a particular purpose, a term requiring the goods to be fit for that particular purpose.

If your sale is to a consumer, these terms cannot be excluded: you must meet the obligations imposed. If your sale is to a person who buys in the course of a business you may be able to exclude them to the extent that it is 'fair and reasonable' to do so. In deciding whether it was fair and reasonable a court would have regard to a range of established criteria. For example, if the seller offers customers a lower price in return for their accepting a lower level of buyer protection, the court may consider this fair and reasonable.

If you sell goods to a consumer, not only is it impossible for you to opt out of the obligations as to description, merchantability and fitness for purpose, but to attempt to do so is an offence punishable by the criminal courts! Unlike the multiple retailers, small businesses do not have the advantage of an in-house legal department to keep an eye on their activities and see that they are acting within the law. Thus, in practice, it is not uncommon for the shopper to come up against attempts by small retailers to unburden themselves of the obligations imposed by the Act. One of the easiest ways to fall foul of the law is a notice displayed in retail premises to the effect that a refund of money cannot be made, perhaps because the goods are sale goods reduced in price. This is not to say that all notices relating to refunds are unlawful, but to ensure that your notice is within the law you need to be aware of what your obligations are. So, what are they?

WHERE THE GOODS HAVE BEEN DESCRIBED

Where there has been what the Sale of Goods Act calls a 'sale by description', the Act implies a term into the contract that the goods supplied will correspond with the description of them made by the seller. When is a sale 'a sale by description'? This certainly includes the situation where the buyer has not seen the goods and is therefore doing the deal relying on a description. We probably buy goods without seeing them more often than we realise: next time you are in a supermarket, look around at the items on display and you will see that most grocery lines are sold in sealed packaging. Since you cannot see the contents of the can, you are relying on the description on the label. If your 'chunks of fresh fruit in thick syrup' turns out to be cat food, there is a breach of the implied term as to description. However, the fact that the buyer has seen the goods does not stop the sale being a sale by description; for example, the description may be of a characteristic which cannot itself be seen. So if a car described by our part-time trader as a 1980 model turns out to comprise the front half of a 1979 welded to the back half of a 1981, there will be a breach of the implied term. Until quite recently it was thought that if anything was said or written about the goods which in some way described them, this would make the transaction a sale by description. However, in recent years the courts have been less willing to label a contract a sale by description if the buyer has not *relied* on the description in making a decision to buy.

Description can include such matters as materials, quantities, measurements, method of packing, weight and ingredients.

A breach by the seller of the implied term as to description, or of the other implied terms, amounts to a breach of contract giving the buyer remedies at civil law, including perhaps the right to sue for compensation through the civil courts. But to secure a sale or score a point over the competition it is tempting for the salesperson to mis-describe what the customer will receive. So Parliament has also made it an offence punishable in the criminal courts to apply, in the course of a business, a false 'trade description' to goods (and services). A 'trade description' only relates to a list of matters set out in the Trades Descriptions Act 1967, although it is quite a long list and includes size, performance, composition and method of manufacture. Our part-time car dealer should be acutely aware of the Act's provisions: the Act is regularly used against car traders who supply cars with false mileages.

MERCHANTABLE QUALITY

Broadly speaking, your goods will meet the requirement of merchantable quality if they are fit for the purpose for which goods of that type are commonly bought. Thus, since shoes are commonly bought for the purpose of walking, if the heel comes off when your buyer wears them for the first time the shoes clearly are *not* of merchantable quality. But the goods only have to be as fit for their common purpose as it is reasonable to expect in the light of the 'relevant circumstances'. These include the price paid for the goods and whether or not they are second-hand.

Defects in the appearance of the goods, if serious enough, can make goods unmerchantable. So, if when you deliver the order, the item boasts a dent which mars its appearance, your customer may be able to claim it is unmerchantable even though it otherwise functions correctly.

What is your position where the customer returns complaining some considerable time after the purchase was made? After all, it may happen that a defect does not appear for some time. Surprisingly, it is not easy to assess the seller's situation. Certainly the goods should be of merchantable quality at the time of sale; therefore if your customer can show that the defect must have been present at that time, even though it has not manifested itself until later, then the customer can succeed in a claim based on merchantability. In one case, a towing hitch bought for a Land-Rover broke due to its defective design, but not until sixteen months after it was fitted: the court held that it was not of merchantable quality.

The fact that the defect is capable of being repaired does not prevent the goods being unmerchantable: it is not for your buyer to put matters right, since they are not getting what they have contracted for.

FITNESS FOR PARTICULAR PURPOSE

Where your customer wants the goods for a particular purpose, provided this is made known to you, the seller, a term will be implied into the deal that the goods shall be fit for that particular purpose. The object of this provision is to cover the situation where a buyer wants goods for a purpose that is not the ordinary purpose for which they are usually bought.

The term is highly relevant where a business supplies exporters who are buying for sale to countries with regulations governing the product, such as safety regulations, or supplying countries with particular climatic conditions. The packaging of your goods may be quite adequate for conditions in the UK, but how would your goods fare while they stood on a Middle East dockside for several days, awaiting onward shipment, under a blazing sun?

This provision will not apply if it would be unreasonable for the buyer to rely on your skill and judgement in the matter. Thus, in the example we have just looked at, if, never having exported your products previously, you are approached by an exporter who is made aware of this, the term may not apply.

CUSTOMER'S REMEDIES FOR BREACH OF THE MAJOR IMPLIED TERMS

Disregard by your business of the implied terms as to description, merchantability and fitness for purpose, means the buyer can reject the goods and refuse to pay for them. This powerful remedy is, however, restricted by a provision in the Act that, unless the contract provides otherwise, the right of rejection is lost once the buyer has accepted the goods. The buyer may, however, still be entitled to compensation for harm suffered in consequence of your breach of contract.

When the trading standards officer calls, or the adviser from Citizens' Advice Bureau telephones, or the buyer's solicitor writes a nasty letter, they are often met with the cry from the honest trader, 'We've done our best – we can't do any more.' It may seem harsh, but if this is true, it is no defence. You must comply strictly with the implied terms as to merchantability and fitness for particular purpose: 'I've done my best' is not good enough.

MANUFACTURER'S LIABILITIES

If you are making the goods you sell, your legal position is much more onerous than if you are merely the seller. It is at the manufacturer's door that liability for unsafe products is laid. Under the Consumer Protection Act 1987, the maker of goods is liable for unsafe products that cause harm to consumers. This is so even though the manufacturer has not been negligent. The consumer who suffers harm – not just personal injury, this could be damage to the consumer's property – can sue the manufacturer without having to prove that the manufacturer failed to take reasonable care. Note here how liability has extended beyond liability to the buyer to include others who use the goods.

Supply of services

If your business is to be one in which you will be carrying out work for your customers, you need to be aware of the provisions of the Supply of Goods and Services Act 1981. We have seen how in a contract for the sale of goods Parliament endeavours to protect the recipient of the goods by implying terms into the contract which the parties have not expressly agreed. Similarly, Parliament has inserted terms in the agreement between supplier and customer for the provision of services. The objective is to establish minimum standards which the recipient of the services can expect to receive. The law does not intervene in every type of service supplied: for example the services of a lawyer in court are expressly excluded! The Act endeavours to deal with these common problems:

● standard of the services provided;

● how long the supplier has to complete the work;

231

● how much the customer is to pay.

THE STANDARD OF YOUR SERVICES

The Act implies a term into the contract that you, the supplier, will carry out your services using reasonable skill and taking reasonable care. This is not an onerous obligation to comply with, representing no more than the minimum standard the reputable business will wish to meet.

TIME FOR COMPLETION

As customers, we know that in some trades it is not uncommon for the parties to leave the date for completion of the services open; that in practice for some types of work it is difficult to gauge exactly how long it will take to carry out the work. If the contract is silent as to a completion date, the Act implies a term that your services shall be rendered within a reasonable time. What is a reasonable time? The only answer that can be given here is that what amounts to a reasonable time depends on all the facts and all the circumstances – a typical lawyer's answer!

THE PRICE PAYABLE

This is another term which in a contract for carrying out work is very much open, much more so than in a contract for the sale of goods. Just as the question of a completion date is often left open because of the problem you will have in gauging how long the work will take, so too is the question of cost. But while you may not be able to agree at the outset the final bill, your practice should be to inform your customer when the agreement is made how you will arrive at the figure. In the absence of either a fixed price or an agreed method for computing the bill, then the customer, relying on a term implied by the Act, need pay only what is reasonable in all the circumstances. This opens the way for the customer to argue about what is reasonable – and almost certainly the customer will not have a proper appreciation of overheads!

Where you will be carrying out work whose nature dictates that you will be supplying customers with a price estimate, rather than a fixed price, choose your words with care. Some tradespeople bandy about the expressions 'estimate' and 'quotation' thinking they are interchangeable. To a lawyer, unless the parties have agreed otherwise, a quotation is for a firm price, whereas an estimate is just that: a prophecy, not a guarantee, of what the price shall be. How accurate should your estimate prove to be? Your customer will have to pay up if the price is within reasonable reach either side of the given figure.

Supplying both goods and services

Perhaps your business will be one in which your customers will receive from you both goods *and* services. An example of where the customer receives both work and materials is the mobile mechanic carrying out a service on the customer's car. The business supplies both labour and the materials used in carrying out the work, such as a new set of plugs. This business is then supplying both goods and services and has accordingly two sets of obligations: responsibility for the services provided and responsibility for the goods supplied.

The responsible and reputable business will meet fully its legal obligations towards customers. Hopefully our brief survey of some areas of law which impinge upon your business operations has whetted your oppetite for this all-important subject.

233

CHAPTER SIXTEEN

Pre-empting the problem

So the time arrives when you are up and running.

More congratulations!

You know there will be both rewards and drawbacks. When you have your own business the rewards belong to you; so too do the problems. The boss is where the buck stops. When you work for somebody else, there is somebody else to take responsibility. The less responsibility you have at work the more you are able to shrug your shoulders.

Your own business: the pride in achievement is yours, the profits are yours, what you have created is yours, the satisfaction is yours, the choices are yours, the interest is yours. And because the business is yours, the problems, disappointments and little aggravations have more impact. Yesterday, you took a phone call at work for a customer cancelling an order; today you took a phone call cancelling an order hard-won by your fragile little business – this one left you with angry disappointment. Less shrugging of the shoulders now.

Drawing on the lessons of practical experience, let us pre-empt or minimise some of the disappointments and aggravation.

It is down to you to look out for your little business.

'The customer is always right'

Hopefully most of the business's customers and suppliers will be honest and reasonable people. It is a fact of life, however, that a percentage of those we have to deal with need particularly careful handling. From time to time you will come across some individual or firm with whom you do not wish to become embroiled. The customer perhaps who, from their attitude, you sense would simply be too much aggravation to deal with; the customer whose demands are too great. In the early months of trading you may feel you have to deal with all and sundry: when you are not yet on your feet, to turn away a customer is a hard choice to make. But unless the financial pressures really leave you no choice, make the choice to bypass Nasty Customer. They are not worth the unpleasantness. Especially if you work from home and they will be disturbing you there.

Since you will not be declining to deal with this person because of their sex or colour, you will not be in breach of the laws against such discrimination: you are otherwise free to choose with whom you do business. I have had a customer say, 'I know my rights – you have to supply me'. He did not know his rights; I did not have to supply him.

Often it will only become clear that we do not wish to deal with a person when we have gone some way down the road with them. How useful it is at a time like this to know some law! How reassuring it is to know at what stage the transaction becomes binding upon us. We know this from our acquaintance with the basic principles of contract law. You will recall at what stage a transaction becomes binding: generally the point at which a party to whom an offer has been made communicates that they are accepting. So if you have decided that you do not want to do business with the other party: do not make them an offer. If it is only after you have made an offer that you realise you would prefer not to tango with them, the general rule is that your offer can be withdrawn at any time up until acceptance. You will recall that you have to notify the other party that you are withdrawing your offer.

'I'll pop a cheque in the post today'

If you are making cash sales over the counter, bad debt will not be a problem. So if you are going to sell free-range eggs from a market stall you are going to experience counting up cash and carrying home a little bag of real money. Then you begin making deliveries of your organic eggs, several trays at a time, to one or two small restaurants. You don't get paid for the last few deliveries, when a notice appears in the restaurant window announcing its temporary closure for re-decoration, and it never reopens.

You can do all the usual things. A solicitor's letter may work, given the right circumstances. Some individuals are alarmed to receive a solicitor's letter and frightened at the prospect of proceedings. But do not overestimate its likely impact: your debtor may have a score of creditors, several solicitor's letters and a really nasty red letter from the collector of taxes. If the first solicitor's letter evokes no response, chasing it up with similar costly letters is probably a waste of money.

A debt collection agency might be more effective and cheaper. Harassment of a debtor may amount to a criminal offence and these experts have a better knowledge than you of how far they may lawfully go to recover your debt. Some of their tactics can be quite sly and may leave a bad taste in the mouth. For example, adopting a business name that includes words such as 'legal' and 'trade protection': the sender's name printed on the envelope, for the postman, family or staff to notice. However, you may not feel so squeamish if, because your customers are not paying you,

236

you are receiving letters from the bank informing you how they are bouncing your standing orders and cheques, and charging you £20 a time for doing so.

It is better to use pre-emptive strategies to minimise your exposure to the risk of bad debt.

We will use as an example a part-time business supplying made-to-measure curtains. The customer receives both services and goods. For the business the labour involved includes measuring up the customer's windows and making· up the fabric into curtains. The material used has to be bought in by the business from a trade supplier.

To keep down bad debt think about the following.

- Cultivate this attitude: don't be afraid to ask for money. Some of us find that asking for money does not come easy. You had assumed the customer would pay you when you delivered the goods, but they make no sign of doing so. Ask for payment – now. It is your money. The customer has had the goods, why should they not pay for them? A form of words you can use is: 'Would you prefer to pay by cash or cheque?' If you are self-conscious about asking for payment, take out a copy of the order or some other piece of paper and scribble on it while asking for payment. But *ask*!

- Wherever possible, try for prepayment. We have to be realistic and recognise that customers may be reluctant to part with their money before they have received the goods: depending on the sum of money involved, prepayment in full may be a deterrent to ordering. In our example of the small business making up curtains, not unnaturally the customer may want to see if the supplier makes a good job of the work before paying: the business is offering a skilled service. Even so, here a request for part payment is entirely reasonable. Help avoid customer doubts and resistance by prefacing

237

your request for a deposit with a brief justification. In this example the salesperson could explain: 'We have to buy in the fabric, of course, and once we have cut it out to your measurements it is no good to anybody else'. Most people are reasonable and would understand this, especially in the case of a small business.

Depending on your margins, you may be able to secure a deposit which would cover your own outgoings in the event of non-payment. With the curtain business, the proprietor is charging the customer for their own labour and for the fabric used: since the fabric is bought in at trade price, this outlay should represent only a proportion of the total charge made to the customer. If the deposit covers the fabric's trade price, in the event of non-payment, while the proprietor remains unrewarded for the work put in, there will be some solace in not having paid out more monies than have been received.

- With certain goods or trades it may be customary to supply on credit: here, do not *assume* that every customer will require credit. If your customers are traders, they are more likely than the public to expect time to pay, but small businesses understand that another small business needs to be paid.

  Big companies may place orders only on the basis of their own standard terms of trading which lay down when they will make payment. Allowing twenty-eight days for payment following receipt of the goods has been the customary practice in many trades, but the recession of the 1980s and early 1990s has seen more buyers endeavouring to extend time for payment. Today a common stipulation in the buyer's standard terms is that they will pay at the end of the month following receipt of the goods: if you deliver the goods early in the month, your buyer will have up to nearly two months' credit. But under your own supplier's terms of trading you may have been granted only twenty-eight days' grace – how will you fund the payment to your supplier before you have yourself been paid for the goods? This is how small businesses build up costly overdrafts. The interest payments and bank charges take huge bites out of your margins.

- Offer a discount for payment with order. This is subject to what has previously been said about causing customers to look at you askance.

  There is no possibility of such a problem with the discount for prompt settlement. Bring this to your customer's attention when submitting the invoice: recite the terms of the discount boldly on the document, e.g. 'You may deduct 2.5% from this sum for payment within 7 days'. Emphasise the saving by working out the discount for the customer, showing the reduced amount the customer has the option of sending.

  Build into your margins an allowance for a percentage of customers to take up this discount. Be prepared for one or two naughty customers to pay after the discount date and deduct the discount anyway.

- What about penalties? What we have just considered are carrots you can offer your customers to encourage prompt payment; late payers should be rewarded with a stick. Your own supplier, especially if a big company, may well have a clause in their terms of trading providing for the payment of interest on accounts paid late. If your customers do not pay you on time, you become the late payer and you are billed interest at, say, 2.5 per cent per month. From time to time I have been asked by small businesses whether they have to pay this when demanded by their suppliers, arguing that it is not the price they agreed to pay. If the supplier's terms include provision for interest, this effectively raises the cost of the goods. The answer is that if the buyer has agreed to purchase on these terms, then this *is* the price they have agreed to pay.

All this brings us to the question: should not your business be protected by its own terms of trading?

Doing business on your terms

In the 1990s probably most medium-sized and big companies do business on the basis of their own standard terms of trading. Huge numbers of small businesses continue to do business without, first, their own set of terms and, secondly, without using, although appropriate, their own comprehensive 'standard form' documentation. When a dispute arises with a customer the terms of the agreement and the obligations of the business will have to be collected together: perhaps from a telephone conversation, or from something said to the customer in the workshop, perhaps from a letter, or from a notice displayed on the premises, possibly from a receipt, or from a note of what has been ordered, written on a page taken from a duplicate book.

Typically, a set of terms of trading will comprise a number of clauses dealing with such matters as delivery, payment, claims for damaged goods or short delivery, carriage, a guarantee. If you are making over the counter cash sales of small-value items, your customers will not expect to read a set of terms of trading before rushing off to catch their bus. Thus, to return to an earlier example, you do not need a set of terms of trading if you are retailing fresh, free-range eggs from your market stall – but when later you expand to supplying in quantity to restaurants...? Doing business on the basis of your own standard set of terms has these advantages.

ADVANTAGE 1

It avoids vague arrangements. You can spell out respective obligations, so that both parties know what they are to receive. It helps avoid customer disappointment. It can also nip disputes in the bud, by enabling you to point a finger at what is stated in writing.

ADVANTAGE 2

Events can occur which make the carrying out of the transaction more difficult: a set of written terms can anticipate such contingencies and make provision for them. You are not released from your obligations merely because it has become more difficult to carry them out. What if you find it difficult to complete the work on time for your customer because the weather is bad?

ADVANTAGE 3

To some extent you will be able to draft the terms so that they are favourable to your interests. How far you can tilt an agreement in your favour is constrained by the need for your terms to be acceptable to your customer.

ADVANTAGE 4

You get the opportunity to include an effective clause limiting, or perhaps even excluding, your legal liability in given circumstances. There is no legal requirement that if you wish to rely on such a clause it needs to be incorporated in a formal set of terms, and in practice such a clause is often to be encountered set out on a notice displayed on the premises, or printed on the back of a ticket handed over to the customer. But the courts are not eager to find that a clause – usually referred to as an exclusion clause – presented in this way is a binding part of the agreement. Exclusion clauses are in any case strictly controlled by law, although their use remains extremely common in business. We have already seen in Chapter 15 that if your business makes sales to consumers you cannot escape the duties imposed upon you as regards description, merchantability and fitness for purpose. Nor can you exclude liability for personal injury that you cause. Other attempts in a standard set of terms to exclude or limit your legal liability will be valid to the extent that they are fair and reasonable, a concept which we met earlier.

WHAT GOES IN YOUR TERMS?

A set of terms, prudently drawn, looks out for the interests of the business. Naturally, factors that need to be taken care of depend upon the nature of your business and your mode of operation: some examples may help to get you thinking along the necessary lines.

- Between the date of the order and the making of delivery is there time enough for your suppliers to increase prices to you? If so, should you not insert a clause in your terms enabling you to pass on this increase to the customer? This is known as a *price variation clause*.

- If your business sells small-value, fast-moving items, the customer who changes their mind after all and doesn't buy half a dozen eggs is an irritation. If your product is a sizeable purchase for customers of whom you have only two or three each week, the telephone call cancelling £250 of made-to-measure curtains can leave you gazing at the phone in despondency. You know from your knowledge of contract law that a clear and definite order accepted by the business has created a binding agreement. But many businesses that deal with the public have made the discovery that a percentage of their customers appear to believe that consumer law enables them to carry on as if they had no obligations themselves, that all the obligations are on one side. One manifestation of this is a belief that they can 'cancel' at whim any transaction they have entered into. But the consumer has only restricted rights of cancellation; primarily, in certain circumstances where credit is being granted to them, or they are buying goods at home. In practice, you may decide to grin and bear a cancellation on the basis that, while it is all very well to insist upon strict legal rights, the customer who is coerced into continuing may be more aggravation than they are worth. But what if, for example, you have yourself already ordered the goods and your supplier does not accept returns? Or what if our curtain maker has already begun cutting out the fabric? While the law of contract may be on your side, if the customer is ignorant of this it may be easier to nip in the bud a purported cancellation by referring the customer to the terms of trading to which they assented and to which they appended their signature.

If cancellations could be a problem for your business, take a deposit from the customer. Customers who have paid no deposit are more likely to cancel.

- *Specification*: spell out what it is the customer is to receive, especially where you are undertaking work for the customer, such as an installation, repairs or maintenance; or where your product is made to order. If you have experience of the particular product or service your new business will be offering, draw on your knowledge to foresee possible complications over specification and forestall them. Does the price include making good damage to the customer's decor incurred

243

during installation? Can our curtain maker guarantee a die match between the fabric sample shown to the customer and the finished product they will receive? If your business will be operating in a trade new to you, be ready to amend your terms of trading/document-ation as you gain experience of problems that arise.

Where is this set of terms to appear? Some businesses incorporate the terms of trading in their catalogue or price list; others set out the terms on a separate sheet of paper, perhaps referring to this in a letter sent to the customer when contact is first made. It is not uncommon for the terms to be set out on the back of an invoice or a delivery note accompanying the goods. You will recall from your knowledge of contract law that the agreement between the parties is complete when acceptance of an offer is com-municated to the party who made the offer. Setting out your terms of trading on a post-agreement document such as an invoice or delivery note is extremely precarious: how can it be said that the other party has agreed to and done business on the basis of these terms if they were not aware of them at the time the agreement was concluded? If you have had regular dealings with the other party, you may be able to contend that they have been fixed with knowledge of your terms via these previous transactions: but if you intend to do business on the basis of your own set of terms, the safer course is to ensure that your customers are supplied with a set of terms at the outset.

The safest course of all is to incorporate them in standard order documentation, completed for each individual order, which is signed by the customer, who is then supplied with a copy. Again, the nature of your business may be such that documentation of this type is inappropriate, but it may be justified by the value of the order or the scale of work you are undertaking, or where work or goods is to a specification which varies from customer to customer.

The documentation could take the form of a formal written agreement; this might, for example, be very appropriate where the obligation is to make regular supplies to the customer, as is the case with our supplier of free-range eggs in their dealings with restaurants. Our earlier example of the business supplying made-to-measure curtains could make use of an order form, incorporating the standard terms of trading and setting out the details of the individual customer's order.

There can be no doubt that the use of such document-ation, signed by the customer, firms up the customer's adhesion to the deal, which in turn helps reduce the number of attempted cancellations. Appropriate prepared docu-mentation helps give your business the appearance of professionalism and efficiency. And the use of appropriate documentation *is* professional and efficient.

Your business documentation
If your customers are members of the general public rather than people in business, bear in mind when designing your documentation that people who are less accustomed to 'paperwork' may be put off signing what to them looks like a legal document. The appearance of the order form, agreement or whatever can be made less daunting by relegating some of the text to the back of the document. The front of the document can be used for insertion of the details relating to the specific transaction. These might include the name and address of the customer, date of delivery, price and details of the goods or services to be supplied. A space for the customer's signature can be left beneath a request to supply the goods or services 'on the terms set out overleaf'. This will help to forestall a later claim that the customer was not aware of the terms; it can be further beefed up by a clause reciting that the customer has read the terms.

Provision can also be made for recording information

245

needed in the various stages of processing the order. This may include:

1. order number?
2. provision for a receipt (e.g. for a deposit)?
3. source of the enquiry?
4. if you are using agents or employees, identity of the individual?
5. method of payment (e.g. cheque or cash)?

Question 3 enables you to monitor the effectiveness of your advertising or other lead-raising method.

In many trades, the trade association makes available standard contract forms for use by its members. This could be a good reason for your joining the National Association of Curtain Retailers, or whatever. You might recoup the cost of membership fees for the first few years from the savings made in not having your own standard document-ation drafted by your lawyer. (*Health warning*: drafting your business's set of terms of trading is not a job for the proprietor! Using the services of a good solicitor is about *saving* money. Regard the expenditure as part of your setting up costs: money laid out now on a set of terms or documentation expertly drawn up is an investment.)

YOUR FINAL TASK

Track down someone who has their own part-time business: ask them what are the main problems they find in running their business.

Then ask this person to remind you of the benefits you also will have from **YOUR OWN PART-TIME BUSINESS!**

APPENDIX A

Useful names and addresses

British Agents Register
24 Mount Parade, Harrogate, North Yorkshire HG1 1PB,
Tel: 0423 560608.

British Franchise Association
75 Bell Street, Henley on Thames, Oxfordshire RG9 2BD,
Tel: 0491 578049.

Rural Development Commission (*formerly Council for Small Industries in Rural Areas*)
141 Castle Street, Salisbury, Wiltshire SP1 3TP,
Tel: 0722 336255.

Small Firms Service
Steel House, Tothill Street, London SW1H 9NF, dial 100
and ask for Freephone Enterprise.

Telecottage Association
c/o Wren Telecottage, Royal Agricultural Centre,
Stoneleigh Park, Warwickshire CV8 2RR,
Tel: 0453 834874.

National Federation of Self-Employed
32 St Annes Road, West Lytham St Annes, Lancashire
FY8 1NY, Tel: 0253 720911.

APPENDIX B

Worthwhile reading

Alistair Crompton, *Do Your Own Advertising* (Hutchinson)
Douglas Foster, *Mastering Marketing* (Macmillan)
Joe Girard with Robert L. Shook, *How to Close Every Sale* (Piatkus)
Christian H. Godefroy and John Clark, *The Complete Time Management System* (Piatkus)
Paul Hague and Peter Jackson, *Do Your Own Market Research* (Kogan Page)
Barrie Hawkins with Grant Bage, *Making Contracts* (Kogan Page)
Barrie Hawkins and Grant Bage, *Think Up a Business* (Rosters)
N. Hill and W. Clement Stone, *Success Through a Positive Mental Attitude* (Thorsons)
Malcom Peel, *Customer Service* (Kogan Page)
Stuart Turner, *Guide to Public Relations* (Thorsons)

INDEX

249